Ireland at a Crossroads

The Triple Lock and Neutrality

TY MURPHY LLB LLM

Copyright © 2025 Ty Murphy LLB LLM

All rights reserved.

ISBN: 979-8-89965-336-0

DALAI LAMA

"Peace does not mean an absence of conflicts; differences will always be there. Peace means solving these differences through peaceful means; through dialogue, education, knowledge, and through humane ways."

CONTENTS

	Foreword	i
	Preface	v
0	Introduction	Pg 1
1	The Birth of Irish Neutrality	Pg 7
2	Geopolitical Challenges to Neutrality	Pg 19
3	Neutrality, Cybersecurity and Hybrid Warfare	Pg 27
4	What is the Triple Lock?	Pg 39
5	How the Triple Lock Works in Practice	Pg 45
6	The Irish Neutrality Movement	Pg 51
7	NATO: Villain or Hero	Pg 59
8	Ireland, NATO and the EU	Pg 77
9	Ireland's Strategic Position as a NATO Member	Pg 85
10	Undersea Cables: Defending Data or Interests?	Pg 91
11	Neutrality in the Face of Economic Coercion	Pg 107
12	Greenland Abandoned: What It Means for Ireland	Pg 117
13	Will NATO Membership Deter Foreign Investment	Pg 129
14	The Irish Neutrality and Sovereignty Act (proposed)	Pg 137
15	The Environmental Cost of Militarization	Pg 145
16	Ireland's Survival in a Global Nuclear War.	Pg 155
17	Casualty Projections in a Conflict Involving Ireland	Pg 163
18	About the Author	Pg 175

Appendices

A: Constitution of Ireland, Relevant Provisions, **p.179**

B: Timeline of Key Events in Irish Neutrality, **p.181**

C: List of Relevant Treaties and Agreements, **p.183**

D: Directory of Organizations and Activists, **p.187**

E: Summary, The North Atlantic Treaty (1949) – Foundational legal document, **p.191**

F: UN Charter – Articles 2(4), 5, and 51, **p.195**

G: UNSC Resolution 1244 (1999) – Mandate for KFOR in Kosovo, **p.199**

H: UNSC Resolution 1973 (2011) – Legal basis for NATO's Libya operation, **p.203**

I: European Court of Human Rights rulings – Cases on CIA black site cooperation, **p.207**

J: Proposed Legal Frameworks and Oversight Mechanisms to Protect Irish Neutrality, **p. 211**

K: Draft Referendum Bill – Irish Neutrality and Sovereignty Amendment, **p.215**

Glossary of Terms, **p.219**

Index, **p.225**

FOREWORD

Ireland has long stood apart—not by force, but by choice. Its policy of neutrality has been more than a strategic position; it has been a profound declaration of national ethos. In a world gripped by military alliances, arms races, and geopolitical entanglements, Ireland chose a different path. It chose peacekeeping over power projection, mediation over militarism, and sovereignty over subordination. And for decades, that path has served the nation well—earning respect in the corridors of the United Nations, saving Irish lives, and preserving the country's moral authority on the global stage.

But today, that path is being redrawn. Ireland's neutrality, once considered a fixed star in its foreign policy constellation, is now being questioned, undermined, and—some argue—relegated to symbolic status. The pressures are both external and internal: from NATO's strategic expansionism, to the EU's burgeoning military architecture, to subtle shifts in language by Irish political elites. Even as public opinion remains firmly supportive of neutrality, state practice is beginning to tell a different story.

This book—*Ireland at a Crossroads: Triple Lock & Neutrality*—is both timely and necessary. With forensic clarity and unwavering principle, Ty Murphy dissects the precarious position in which Ireland now finds itself. He does not rely on abstractions or sentimentality. Instead, he offers a detailed, rigorous, and deeply human account of how neutrality has been upheld, where it has faltered, and why it must now be fortified.

At the heart of this analysis lies the **Triple Lock**—a unique legal and political safeguard that has served as the final checkpoint before Irish troops can be deployed abroad. Under this mechanism, the deployment of military personnel requires the approval of three separate entities: the United Nations, the Irish government, and the Dáil Éireann. It is, in essence, a democratic firewall against the quiet slide into conflict.

But as Murphy reveals, this firewall is being chipped away. There are those who argue that the UN element is outdated or that the Triple Lock is cumbersome in a time of fast-moving global crises. These arguments may be cloaked in the language of modernization or strategic flexibility, but their effect is clear: to loosen the bonds of democratic accountability and expose Ireland to the gravitational pull of foreign wars.

Yet Murphy's work goes beyond critique. He offers an antidote to drift. This is not merely a book of diagnosis; it is a blueprint for recovery and renewal. He makes the compelling case for a national referendum to enshrine neutrality in the Constitution—transforming it from a political convention into a legal imperative. He outlines the mechanisms through which neutrality could be safeguarded in law, monitored by an independent oversight body, and protected from the influence of lobbyists, foreign defense contractors, and transient political winds.

Just as crucially, he reminds us that neutrality is not just the concern of diplomats or legal scholars—it is a civic responsibility. This book invites every Irish reader to re-engage with a national principle that, if lost, may never be reclaimed. Through its chapters, we hear the echoes of historical defiance, the pragmatism of small-state survival, and the voices of the people who, in poll after poll, have affirmed a clear and steady message: Ireland must remain a neutral nation.

Murphy's exploration of NATO, the EU's Permanent Structured Cooperation (PESCO), and the use of Shannon Airport as a logistics hub for foreign militaries reveals a sobering pattern—one of gradual erosion masked as administrative necessity. These are not isolated events. They are indicators of a creeping alignment with military blocs that may ultimately demand more than Ireland is willing—or able—to give.

The book also engages with the economic and political blackmail used by global superpowers. It confronts the fallout of the Trump-era tariffs and warns against the weaponization of trade, data, and investment as tools to bend Ireland into submission. Here, neutrality is framed not just as a foreign policy issue, but as a matter of national survival—economic, political, and moral. This is not a dry policy text. It is a fierce, reasoned, and vital work. It challenges assumptions, exposes contradictions, and, most importantly, offers hope. It reminds us that neutrality is not weakness. It is strength guided by wisdom. It is not inaction. It is principled restraint. And in a world tilting toward renewed Cold War dynamics, proxy conflicts, and ideological suppression, Ireland's ability to stand apart may become one of its most powerful assets.

"Ireland at a Crossroads: Triple Lock & Neutrality" is a necessary book for a pivotal moment. It equips citizens with the tools to understand the stakes and the courage to act. Whether you are a policymaker, an academic, a peace

activist, or a concerned citizen, this book is your invitation to re-enter the conversation about what kind of Ireland we want to be—and what we are willing to defend.

Let the world rush to arms. Let great powers jostle for dominance. Let others trade sovereignty for security illusions. Ireland must remain different. It must remain neutral. And this book shows us why—and how.

David D Lewis
Solicitor

PREFACE

Ireland's soul is not found in its borders or its GDP—but in the choices it makes when the world demands obedience and it chooses independence instead.

Neutrality has long been one of the most dignified pillars of Irish identity. It is not a slogan, nor a relic of the past—it is a moral compass, a political stance, and a promise to ourselves and the world. It says that Ireland does not fight other people's wars. It says that sovereignty matters. It says that peace is a position of strength, not weakness.

But that compass is spinning.

When I set out to write *Ireland at a Crossroads: The Triple Lock & Neutrality*, it was not out of academic curiosity—it was out of deep personal conviction that something essential is being lost. Neutrality, once a clear and principled stance, is now being blurred at the edges by quiet concessions and clever legal footwork. Our government debates neutrality in abstract terms, even as planes refuel in Shannon en route to illegal wars, and new EU military pacts are signed without public mandate. We are told these changes are minor, administrative, technical. But they are not. They are strategic. And they are eroding the very foundation of Ireland's independent foreign policy.

At the heart of this erosion is the **Triple Lock**—a democratic mechanism that ensures Ireland cannot deploy troops abroad without the consent of the United Nations, the Irish Government, and the Dáil. This safeguard was never an obstacle to Ireland's engagement with the world; it was the very thing that allowed our peacekeepers to operate abroad with moral clarity and legal legitimacy. Today, that mechanism is under threat. There are those who say it is outdated, that it weakens Ireland's response to crises. But I believe the opposite: removing the Triple Lock is not about flexibility—it's about surrender. Surrendering control, surrendering neutrality, and surrendering the will of the Irish people to foreign agendas.

This book is my attempt to speak directly to that threat—with facts, history, and unflinching analysis. It is part of the Irish Neutrality Series, a body of work I have committed myself to as both a legal scholar and a citizen deeply concerned with the direction this country is taking. My aim is not to romanticize neutrality, but to explain why it matters—legally, politically, and morally—and how close we are to losing it.

Ireland is being quietly drawn into the orbit of military alliances and power blocs. Through the EU's **Permanent Structured Cooperation (PESCO)**, Ireland is entering defense agreements that many citizens have never heard of. Through NATO-aligned intelligence sharing and joint operations, Ireland risks becoming a silent partner in wars it never chose to fight. Behind closed doors, lobbyists for arms manufacturers and foreign interests are shaping security policies that few elected officials seem willing to challenge.

I do not believe the Irish public supports this direction. Poll after poll shows the people value neutrality. They understand that it has kept Ireland respected and safe. They see through the fiction that neutrality makes us weak or irrelevant. But their voices are not being heard—because the debate is too often kept behind parliamentary curtains, obscured by technicalities and softened by euphemisms.

That's why this book exists.

Yes, it covers the **Triple Lock**—how it works, why it matters, and how its removal would change Ireland forever. But it also goes further, examining the deeper forces shaping Irish defense policy today. It looks at **Shannon Airport**, where neutrality is violated not in word but in practice. It looks at the **EU's creeping militarization** and the question of whether the Irish Defence Forces are being prepared for a future that the public has not endorsed. It considers the growing reality that Ireland is no longer viewed as a neutral nation by the rest of the world—but as an emerging member of a European defense bloc.

Still, this is not a book of despair. It is a book of strategy, of urgency, and of hope.

I offer concrete proposals, including a **national referendum** to enshrine neutrality in the Constitution—making it not merely a policy but a legal principle immune to political whim. I explore whether a **Neutrality and Sovereignty Act** could serve as a shield against backdoor militarization. I discuss **grassroots activism**, and how citizens—ordinary citizens—can reclaim the conversation and make neutrality not just a historical legacy, but a modern force for peace and independence.

This book is short by design. It is meant to be accessible. It is written for citizens, not just specialists. Because neutrality is not the property of politicians—it is the inheritance of the people. And whether we keep it or lose it will depend not on what is said in government chambers, but on what is demanded by those outside them.

Ireland is at a crossroads. We can take the path of integration into someone else's army, someone else's war, someone else's agenda. Or we can choose the path we know: independence, peace, and clarity of purpose. Not isolation, but integrity.

My hope is that this book helps us make the right choice.

—

Ty Murphy, LLB, LLM

INTRODUCTION

Who Can Be Trusted When the World Is Burning? The Case for Irish Neutrality in an Age of Global Betrayals

"Those who make peaceful revolution impossible will make violent revolution inevitable." – **John F. Kennedy**

Ireland stands at a crossroads—not for the first time in its long and hard-fought history, but perhaps at its most dangerous. Not because of tanks on the border or an invading fleet on the horizon, but because of subtler forces: economic coercion masquerading as diplomacy, military integration cloaked in bureaucratic language, and alliances that once promised protection now demanding obedience. Neutrality, long the moral compass and geopolitical backbone of Ireland's foreign policy, is under siege. This book is a clarion call to protect it—not as a relic of the past, but as a strategic, legal, and philosophical necessity for the 21st century.

We live in an era where the very concept of trust in global affairs has been undermined. Can Ireland trust Donald Trump's America, a nation where policy whiplash is now the norm, where allies are threatened with tariffs and adversaries courted with spectacle? Can Ireland place its fate in the hands of a European Union increasingly drifting toward centralized military command, championing hate speech laws that stifle dissent and erode democratic discourse? Can it find safety under NATO's umbrella, an alliance that has time and again acted outside of international law—from Yugoslavia to Libya—and increasingly demands not solidarity but subservience?

Or, amid this storm, is Ireland's safest course to trust what it already knows? A tested path. A constitutional conscience. A people who have always prized peace over power, diplomacy over domination, independence over entanglement. That path is neutrality.

"Peace cannot be kept by force; it can only be achieved by understanding." – **Albert Einstein**

Irish neutrality is not a passive refusal to engage with the world—it is an active moral stance, earned through blood, hardship, and hard choices. It is not naïveté or nostalgia. It is the discipline to say "no" when the world rushes to war. It is the courage to offer aid when others drop bombs. It is the foresight to remain unbound to the war machines of others so that Ireland may be free to speak truth, negotiate peace, and uphold international law when others abandon it.

From the moment Ireland cast off the chains of empire, it faced a choice: to become a subordinate within someone else's alliance, or to stand as a sovereign beacon of peace. Again and again, Ireland chose the latter. From the Emergency during World War II to the era of Cold War polarities, Ireland held firm to a policy of military non-alignment, all the while contributing soldiers to UN peacekeeping missions in some of the world's most dangerous flashpoints—from the Congo to the Golan Heights. It did not stand idle; it stood tall.

"The real and lasting victories are those of peace, and not of war." – **Ralph Waldo Emerson**

This book does not ask the reader to admire neutrality out of sentimentality. It asks you to understand it as a vital doctrine of statecraft. A doctrine under threat. The post–Cold War world is not a safer one—it is a more complex and chaotic one. The battlefield has expanded into cyberspace, media, currency, and lawfare. Militarization now wears a suit and sits at negotiation tables. Ireland's neutrality, if not formally protected and actively defended, can be eroded not with bombs but with quiet signatures and semantic loopholes.

Each chapter of this book peels back the layers of that erosion and offers, not just critique, but a pathway forward. We begin with the legal and cultural origins of neutrality, tracing its roots in Irish history, Bunreacht na hÉireann, and Ireland's post-colonial psyche. We examine the forces threatening neutrality today: cyberwarfare, hybrid tactics, EU military ambitions, and the crumbling of transatlantic norms. The Triple Lock, long held as a safeguard against unilateral military action, is dissected in theory and in practice—revealing both its virtues and its vulnerabilities.

"True patriotism is not about waving a flag or blindly obeying the state; it is about holding your country to its highest ideals." – **Barack Obama**

We explore the growing divide between public sentiment and elite decision-making, highlighting the Irish Neutrality Movement and the strong polling data that consistently shows popular support for staying out of NATO and foreign wars. We scrutinize NATO not only as a political body but as a legal actor whose history includes multiple violations of international humanitarian law, most without UN authorization. If NATO is a shield, one must ask: who decides where and when it is raised, and against whom?

Chapters further examine how Ireland's unique geostrategic position—sitting at the western edge of Europe, hosting key undersea cables, and serving as a tech and pharmaceutical hub—makes it both valuable and vulnerable. We analyze how Shannon Airport's quiet repurposing into a military logistics node violates international law and contradicts Ireland's claimed neutrality. We review how financial warfare—like the 2025 Trump tariffs—can be used to force alignment, with multinational corporations and digital infrastructure caught in the crossfire.

The consequences are not theoretical. In a world inching toward nuclear brinkmanship, this book offers sober projections of what a major war involving NATO might mean for Irish civilians—whether Ireland is a member or not. We explore emergency preparedness, nuclear fallout scenarios, and the ethical implications of being a small country used by larger ones for strategic advantage.

"He who accepts evil without protesting against it is really cooperating with it." – **Martin Luther King Jr.**

At its core, this book is not just an analysis. It is a defense. A defense of conscience in foreign policy. A defense of the small state's right to choose peace. A defense of the Irish people's historical wisdom in resisting the seductive pull of military alliances that often lead to war without justice.

Yet it is also a vision. We present a proposed Irish Neutrality and Sovereignty Act to enshrine military neutrality into the Constitution, closing loopholes and empowering the public to decide—by referendum—whether Ireland joins foreign conflicts. We call for a standing oversight body to review all government activities that might infringe upon neutrality, including foreign lobbying, military transits, and intelligence-sharing agreements.

Neutrality is not inertia. It is intention. In a world convulsing under the weight of new empires, old ambitions, and perpetual war, Ireland's path must remain guided by its own hand, not by pressure from Washington, Brussels, or London.

"The only thing necessary for the triumph of evil is for good men to do nothing." – **Edmund Burke**

So we return to the question: Who can be trusted? The answer may be that in this new world disorder, trust must begin at home. Trust in our history. Trust in our Constitution. Trust in the will of the people who have, again and again, affirmed that neutrality is not only who we were—it is who we must be if we are to remain free.

As you read this book, you are not just encountering facts and arguments. You are engaging in a national conversation about identity, ethics, and the future of Irish sovereignty. This is the first battle—not one fought with weapons but with words, clarity, and conviction.

May it not be the last.

1

THE BIRTH OF IRISH NEUTRALITY

The roots of Irish neutrality trace back not to a single political decision, but to a constellation of historical experiences, national aspirations, and ideological convictions. By the early 20th century, Ireland's political landscape had been shaped by centuries of resistance to imperial rule and a deep desire for self-determination. The formation of the Irish Free State in 1922 marked not only political independence from Britain but a psychological rupture from the global power structures that had dominated Irish life for generations.

In the years following independence, neutrality emerged less as a formal doctrine and more as an instinctive reaction to the complex international order. Ireland's early leaders were acutely aware of the fragility of their new state and the divisiveness of foreign entanglements. The Irish people, still reeling from internal conflict, viewed foreign wars, particularly those involving former colonial powers, with suspicion. There was little appetite to become embroiled in distant imperial conflicts, especially those led by Britain, whose legacy in Ireland remained painful.

This foundational period established the psychological underpinning of Irish neutrality: a policy grounded not in pacifism but in pragmatism and national sovereignty. The small and recovering state simply could not afford the political, military, or economic costs of aligning itself with larger blocs, particularly as global tensions began to escalate in the 1930s.

The Irish Civil War, though internal in nature, played a formative role in shaping Ireland's future stance on neutrality. The conflict, fought between pro-Treaty and anti-Treaty forces over the Anglo-Irish Treaty of 1921, was not merely a political schism—it was a violent rupture that left deep scars across Irish society. The trauma of fratricidal conflict had profound consequences for how Ireland viewed the use of force, military alliances, and foreign involvement in national affairs.

While the war itself was not one of neutrality, its aftermath helped embed the principle into the political psyche. One of the enduring legacies of the conflict was a widespread aversion to militarism. The new state, having emerged from both the War of Independence and the Civil War, was reluctant to maintain a large standing army or to pursue military solutions to international problems. The focus was on reconstruction, reconciliation, and the creation of a distinct Irish identity separate from both Britain and continental Europe.

Moreover, there was an unspoken consensus among many political leaders—across the ideological spectrum—that Ireland should avoid importing foreign conflicts into its fragile domestic order. International entanglements, especially military ones, risked reopening wounds that had not yet healed.

The Civil War also crystallized the importance of sovereignty in Irish political culture. Both sides in the conflict had invoked the principle of Irish independence, albeit with different visions of how it should be achieved. This focus on autonomy would, in time, evolve into a defensive reflex against alliance politics, especially those that might limit Ireland's freedom to act independently on the global stage.

Thus, while the Civil War was a domestic tragedy, its long-term impact was to push Ireland toward a cautious, non-aligned foreign policy—one that sought peace, stability, and self-determination above all.

Of all the formative tests of Irish neutrality, none was more consequential than the Second World War. Known in Ireland as "The Emergency," the years from 1939 to 1945 defined the Republic's modern foreign policy. Led by Taoiseach Éamon de Valera, the Irish government declared neutrality on September 2, 1939—one day after Germany invaded Poland. While the global conflict threatened to engulf all of Europe, Ireland remained officially non-aligned.

This decision was far from simple. The British government, under immense wartime pressure, repeatedly sought Irish cooperation. Churchill's cabinet proposed offering Irish unity—ending partition—in exchange for Irish entry into the war. Though some in Dublin were tempted by the prospect, de Valera held firm. He understood that entering the war on Britain's side would not only divide the country politically but also compromise the fragile sovereignty Ireland had secured after centuries of struggle.

The choice to remain neutral was rooted in both practicality and principle. Ireland lacked the military resources to defend itself in a large-scale war. Its geographic position made it strategically valuable to both Axis and Allied powers, and any overt alignment could have made it a target for invasion. Moreover, de Valera believed that Ireland's role as a neutral state could contribute to peace in the long term, and that Irish soldiers should not be conscripted to fight for imperial interests—especially when many still remembered British rule with bitterness.

Nonetheless, neutrality did not mean isolation. The Irish government quietly shared intelligence with the Allies and allowed British aircraft to fly over certain corridors of Irish airspace, known as the "Donegal Corridor." At the same time, German diplomats and intelligence officers were permitted to remain in Dublin, and Axis planes that crashed in Ireland were interred. Irish soldiers who deserted the army to fight with Allied forces were not celebrated, but punished after the war.

De Valera's unwavering commitment to neutrality came under sharp criticism—especially after he offered condolences to the German ambassador upon Hitler's death in 1945. While many saw this as a diplomatic misstep, it was consistent with his absolute interpretation of neutrality: Ireland was not to take sides.

The Emergency cemented neutrality as not just policy, but identity. It was during this time that neutrality became associated with independence, sovereignty, and a refusal to be drawn into wars decided by great powers. It was also the first major proof that Ireland, despite outside pressure, would chart its own course.

Following the Second World War, the international system quickly fractured into the ideological standoff of the Cold War. The United States and the Soviet Union emerged as rival superpowers, drawing much of the world into two competing camps. In this polarized environment, Ireland's continued commitment to neutrality was tested anew. Yet, rather than yielding to bloc politics, Ireland reaffirmed its non-alignment—refusing to join NATO, declining to align with the Warsaw Pact, and positioning itself as a neutral European democracy.

Ireland's exclusion from NATO in the late 1940s and early 1950s was not simply a matter of being overlooked. NATO membership required a commitment to collective defense, which would have violated Ireland's constitutional dedication to peace and its longstanding policy of non-alignment. Moreover, joining NATO would likely have required concessions on partition, particularly as Northern Ireland remained firmly within the United Kingdom—a NATO founding member. Successive Irish governments were unwilling to legitimize partition by joining an alliance that included the UK while Ireland remained divided.

Instead, Ireland leaned into its neutrality. At the United Nations, where it became a member in 1955, Ireland began to build a reputation as a principled advocate for nuclear disarmament, decolonization, and peacekeeping. Figures such as Frank Aiken, Ireland's first Minister for External Affairs, championed a foreign policy that emphasized moral leadership over military alignment. In 1968, Ireland played a central role in negotiating the Treaty on the Non-Proliferation of Nuclear Weapons (NPT), helping to codify the global consensus against nuclear escalation.

At home, the policy of neutrality enjoyed widespread support. The memory of The Emergency was still fresh, and there remained little appetite for entanglement in superpower rivalries. Public opinion reflected deep unease about the Vietnam War, the arms race, and the military-industrial complex dominating Western strategy.

Still, Irish neutrality during the Cold War was pragmatic. The government maintained strong diplomatic and economic ties with Western Europe and the United States. Ireland benefited from U.S. investment, participated in European integration, and contributed troops to UN peacekeeping missions. But it always did so on its own terms, avoiding entanglement in military alliances while embracing a multilateral order based on peaceful cooperation.

This dual track—economic alignment with the West and political non-alignment in military affairs—became a defining feature of Irish foreign policy. The Cold War affirmed what The Emergency had begun: neutrality was not isolationism, but active independence.

Ireland's neutrality, while shaped by its unique historical and political context, is part of a broader European tradition. Throughout the 20th century, several other countries chose the path of neutrality, either formally or through long-standing policy decisions. While each case differs, comparative analysis helps highlight both the shared logic and the distinctiveness of Ireland's approach.

Switzerland is perhaps the world's most recognized neutral state. Its neutrality dates back to the early 19th century and was formalized at the Congress of Vienna in 1815. Switzerland's neutrality is codified in its constitution and has allowed it to avoid major conflict involvement for over two centuries. Its neutrality is underpinned by a robust military deterrent, compulsory national service, and a diplomatic policy of non-interference. Despite being geographically central in Europe, Switzerland has stayed out of NATO and the EU, offering itself instead as a mediator and host for international diplomacy.

Austria offers a different model. Following the Second World War, Austria declared its permanent neutrality in 1955 as part of the State Treaty with the Allied powers, a condition for the withdrawal of occupying Soviet and Western forces. Austrian neutrality is enshrined in its constitution, making it legally binding and politically entrenched. Like Ireland, Austria joined the European Union in 1995 but did so without joining NATO. It participates in the EU's Common Security and Defence Policy (CSDP), but maintains a strict policy of non-alignment and non-membership in military alliances.

Sweden historically pursued neutrality as a pragmatic policy after avoiding involvement in the world wars. Although its neutrality was never constitutionally mandated, it became a core part of national identity. Like Ireland, Sweden contributed heavily to UN peacekeeping and emphasized diplomacy, humanitarian aid, and disarmament. However, the Russian invasion of Ukraine in 2022 led Sweden to abandon decades of neutrality and apply for NATO membership, marking a dramatic shift driven by security concerns and regional solidarity.

Finland, sharing a long border with Russia, maintained a policy of neutrality and non-alignment during the Cold War through a complex balancing act known as "Finlandization"—maintaining independence while avoiding confrontation with the Soviet Union. Like Sweden, Finland was a strong supporter of international law, peacekeeping, and multilateral cooperation. But in 2023, faced with renewed Russian aggression, Finland joined NATO. This decision, while seen as a loss of neutrality, was viewed domestically as a necessity for national defense.

Compared to these states, Ireland's neutrality has been less formalized but equally resilient. Unlike Switzerland and Austria, Ireland's neutrality is not enshrined in its constitution. Yet it has endured, largely due to public support, historical memory, and a national identity shaped by anti-colonialism and independence. Ireland's version of neutrality is also characterized by a dual commitment: rejecting military alliances while embracing humanitarianism, development, and international cooperation through the UN and EU.

The experiences of these nations demonstrate that neutrality is not a static concept. It evolves with threat perceptions, political change, and public sentiment. Ireland's neutrality, while rooted in national experience, has always been part of a wider European discourse on how small states can maintain sovereignty, security, and moral agency in a dangerous world.

Ireland's entry into the European Economic Community (EEC) in 1973 marked a transformative moment in its modern history. It was the beginning of full economic integration into Western Europe, offering access to markets, structural funds, and political capital. However, even at this early stage, questions arose about whether neutrality could survive Ireland's deepening ties with a regional bloc increasingly interested in developing common security and defense policies.

In the early years of EEC membership, neutrality was largely a non-issue. The EEC was, after all, an economic project. Defense remained firmly under the remit of NATO, to which Ireland did not belong. Nevertheless, Irish policymakers were aware that full political integration might someday raise conflicts between neutrality and collective EU action—especially if the EEC were to evolve into a more explicitly political and security-based union.

Through the 1980s and 1990s, this tension became more pronounced. As the EEC transformed into the European Union under the Maastricht Treaty of 1992, it began to develop foreign policy structures, including the Common Foreign and Security Policy (CFSP). Irish participation in these discussions was careful and measured. Ireland supported EU diplomacy, development, and peacebuilding efforts, but consistently reiterated its non-alignment and refusal to participate in a mutual defense pact.

The Treaty of Amsterdam In 1997 and the Treaty of Nice in 2001 introduced new security dimensions into EU policy, especially in relation to crisis management and military coordination under the European Security and Defence Policy (ESDP). Irish neutrality came under renewed scrutiny during these negotiations, with critics warning that the evolving EU architecture risked dragging Ireland into a de facto security alliance. The Irish government responded by emphasizing that its participation in EU security frameworks would remain within strict limits: no standing army, no mutual defense obligation, and full respect for the country's traditional military neutrality.

Despite this cautious line, public concern persisted—especially after the Lisbon Treaty (2009) created a formal mutual defense clause under Article 42.7 of the Treaty on European Union. Ireland negotiated a formal legal opt-out, reaffirming that its neutrality would not be compromised. This move underscored a deeper truth: even within the EU, neutrality had to be actively defended, and not just assumed.

The Irish approach to the EEC and EU has therefore been one of selective integration—full participation in economic and diplomatic aspects, but consistent resistance to military entanglement. This strategy, though not without friction, has allowed Ireland to maintain its identity as a neutral state while benefiting from European solidarity.

While the Second World War is often seen as the crucible of Irish neutrality, the Spanish Civil War (1936–1939) offers an earlier and often overlooked case study. The conflict, fought between the leftist Republican government and the right-wing Nationalists under General Francisco Franco, posed a profound challenge for many European states—including Ireland. Though officially neutral, Ireland's domestic reaction to the Spanish conflict revealed the complex relationship between neutrality, ideology, and national identity.

At the governmental level, Ireland maintained a formal stance of non-intervention. The Irish Free State adhered to the Non-Intervention Agreement promoted by Britain and France, which aimed to prevent the conflict from becoming a proxy war between Fascist and Communist powers. However, neutrality was difficult to enforce domestically, and Ireland—like many other nations—was deeply divided in its sympathies.

Éamon de Valera's government, while officially neutral, came under pressure from both pro-Republican and pro-Franco elements within Irish society. The Catholic Church, which wielded significant influence in 1930s Ireland, viewed the Spanish conflict through a religious lens. Many Irish clergy saw Franco as a defender of Catholicism against an anti-clerical and Marxist threat. Their rhetoric resonated with a large segment of the population, helping to shape a public mood sympathetic to the Nationalists.

This support took concrete form when approximately 700 Irish volunteers, led by former IRA chief-of-staff Eoin O'Duffy, traveled to Spain to fight on Franco's side as part of the "Irish Brigade." Though the Irish government did not officially sanction their departure, it took limited steps to prevent it, illustrating the blurry boundaries between formal neutrality and ideological alignment.

At the same time, a smaller number of Irish volunteers fought on behalf of the Spanish Republic. These individuals, many of them socialists, trade unionists, or members of the IRA's left wing, joined the International Brigades. Their presence, though far smaller in number, offered a counterpoint to the dominant narrative and underscored the domestic divisions within Ireland over the war in Spain.

Ultimately, the Spanish Civil War exposed the limitations of Irish neutrality when confronted with ideological conflict. While the state remained officially non-aligned, popular sentiment and unofficial action told a more complicated story. The episode was an early test of Ireland's ability to separate policy from passion—one it passed only partially. Nevertheless, the government's decision to stay out of the conflict formally helped lay the groundwork for the more robust neutrality it would adopt in the years to come.

Irish neutrality did not emerge fully formed. It was not the product of a single document or legal doctrine, but the cumulative result of historical trauma, political pragmatism, and moral calculation. What began as a defensive posture in the aftermath of internal conflict and external domination gradually evolved into a defining feature of the Irish state.

From the Irish Civil War through the Second World War and into the Cold War, neutrality became the means by which Ireland asserted its independence—not only from Britain, but from the coercive logic of great power politics. While neutrality has often been treated as a moral high ground, in Ireland it has also been a strategic necessity. Lacking the resources to shape global events, Ireland instead chose to limit its exposure to them. That was not weakness; it was wisdom.

The comparison with other neutral nations further highlights this point. Switzerland's armed neutrality, Austria's constitutional commitment, Sweden and Finland's post-WWII pragmatism—each provides a different model. Ireland's path has been less formal, more fluid, and shaped uniquely by its anti-colonial identity. Yet in all cases, neutrality has been used to safeguard sovereignty and to carve out space for diplomatic relevance.

Legal underpinnings matter. While Ireland's neutrality is not directly embedded in the Constitution, Article 29 provides a framework for independent foreign policy and peaceful cooperation. In practice, every step toward deeper EU integration or global security cooperation has required careful negotiation to preserve this principle. The Lisbon Treaty opt-out on defense, for example, shows that neutrality must be actively defended, not merely assumed.

The challenge for contemporary Ireland is ensuring that neutrality continues to serve the public interest in an increasingly polarized world. As explored in later chapters, military alliances like NATO and EU defense initiatives like PESCO are testing the limits of Ireland's independence. The push from both Washington and Brussels is real, and the pressures of hybrid war, cyber threats, and economic coercion make neutrality more complex than ever.

Yet, complexity does not mean irrelevance. In a world that appears to be dividing once more into competing blocs, Ireland's neutrality offers a rare and valuable alternative. It positions the country as a mediator, a peacebuilder, and a trusted host. It is precisely because neutrality is hard to maintain that it is worth maintaining. It is not a luxury of the past—it is a safeguard for the future.

Neutrality, then, is not merely about avoiding war. It is about preserving the ability to make decisions that reflect the nation's values, interests, and identity—free from foreign dictates or entangling obligations. It is the clearest expression of Ireland's hard-won sovereignty, and the most effective instrument for projecting its unique voice in global affairs.

In that sense, the birth of Irish neutrality is not a closed chapter. It is a continuing story—one that must be told, debated, and defended, again and again.

2

GEOPOLITICAL CHALLENGES TO NEUTRALITY

Ireland's geographical position places it on the western periphery of Europe, acting as a crucial Atlantic outpost that many major powers view with strategic interest. Situated between North America and the European continent, Ireland's airspace and maritime zones intersect with critical transatlantic shipping lanes, communication cables, and surveillance corridors. Historically, this position has made Ireland a logistical pivot—used by Britain during both World Wars, and monitored closely by NATO ever since.

Despite its official neutrality, Ireland finds itself under indirect geopolitical pressure from surrounding military alliances. U.S. military use of Shannon Airport for refuelling operations—especially in the context of Middle Eastern wars—has already blurred lines between passive neutrality and de facto cooperation. While the Irish government insists on a policy of non-engagement in conflicts, the hosting of foreign military logistics, even indirectly, chips away at this stance.

This strategic position is also valuable in terms of undersea infrastructure. A significant portion of the world's submarine communication cables, which carry global internet traffic, come ashore in Ireland. As noted in **Chapter 10: Undersea Cables – Defending Data or Interests?**, these cables make Ireland a cybersecurity linchpin. But they also represent a vulnerability. As hybrid warfare grows, cyberattacks and sabotage to these cables could draw Ireland into the centre of military retaliation or geopolitical standoffs.

From a geopolitical perspective, larger powers may not always respect Ireland's declared neutrality when they see strategic advantage in its territory. In any broader European conflict—especially involving NATO or Russia—Ireland's Atlantic position could be exploited for surveillance, air patrols, or even as a defensive buffer by one side or another, regardless of Ireland's consent.

Under international law, neutrality entails refraining from participating in armed conflict and denying belligerents the use of national territory. However, the Hague Conventions (1907) and customary international law recognize that neutral countries have sovereign rights to control their airspace, maritime zones, and land. If a neutral nation permits repeated military use of its territory, it risks being seen as a "non-belligerent ally," voiding its neutral protections. The Irish use of Shannon Airport may thus risk contravening Articles 1 and 5 of the Hague Convention V on the Rights and Duties of Neutral Powers and Persons in Case of War on Land.

Over the past two decades, there has been a marked increase in reports of foreign military vessels and aircraft entering Irish sovereign zones—

especially by Russia and NATO states. Russian naval manoeuvres off the southwest coast, particularly near undersea cables, have raised alarm in the Irish Defence Forces. Meanwhile, NATO aircraft frequently traverse Irish-controlled airspace without consistent adherence to Irish protocol, often citing regional agreements or the need for rapid response drills.

Ireland, unlike many of its neighbours, lacks a robust radar and air defence infrastructure. It is reliant on a 2015 bilateral agreement with the United Kingdom allowing the RAF to police Irish airspace in the event of an emergency—an arrangement which many see as an informal erosion of sovereignty. In times of crisis, it is likely that NATO would assume control over Irish skies, regardless of parliamentary consent.

Fishing communities, coastal environmental groups, and even the Department of Foreign Affairs have raised repeated concerns about unauthorized exercises and the proximity of warships to offshore energy sites and communication networks. Irish military capacity is limited—currently with fewer than 10 operational naval vessels and a defence budget among the lowest per capita in the EU.

The strategic ambiguity exploited by militarized powers operating in and around Irish territory exposes the limits of soft neutrality. Without sufficient surveillance, air defence, and maritime enforcement, Ireland's neutrality is vulnerable not only to violation but also to irrelevance.

Article 2(4) of the UN Charter prohibits the threat or use of force against the territorial integrity of any state. Furthermore, under UNCLOS (United Nations Convention on the Law of the Sea), Ireland maintains exclusive rights within its territorial sea (12 nautical miles) and its Exclusive Economic Zone (EEZ). However, enforcement capacity is key. Failure to monitor and deter incursions could result in legal grey zones, where repeated unauthorized foreign presence becomes normalized, undermining both sovereignty and neutrality protections.

The geopolitical landscape is shifting rapidly toward outer space, and neutrality is being redefined in real time. Ireland is a signatory to the Outer Space Treaty of 1967, which declares that space shall be used exclusively for peaceful purposes. But space today is becoming increasingly militarized—with satellite constellations being deployed for surveillance, missile defence, and communication by major powers like the U.S., China, and Russia.

Private companies with state links, such as SpaceX, are launching thousands of satellites with dual-use capabilities. These systems can aid navigation and emergency response, but they also serve real-time military operations and targeting systems. Ireland, by virtue of its geolocation and participation in various EU space and cybersecurity programs, risks entanglement in the militarized web of space activity.

For instance, Irish telecommunications firms and universities are increasingly collaborating in space innovation and satellite technology. While these are framed as scientific or commercial partnerships, they often overlap with European Defence Agency (EDA) initiatives. Under PESCO (Permanent Structured Cooperation), Ireland participates in space situational awareness and cyber defence projects, which some legal scholars argue already violate Ireland's traditional stance of military neutrality.

Neutrality in space presents another layer of complexity—there are no "neutral orbits." Satellites over Ireland's skies may be used to spy, target, or transmit military data, and Irish firms involved in satellite networks may become pressure points during conflicts.

Ireland is bound by the Outer Space Treaty, but legal enforcement in space is still nascent. Articles I and IV forbid national appropriation and require the peaceful use of celestial bodies. However, the Treaty does not ban the militarization of all satellite functions. Furthermore, under Article VI, states are responsible for national activities in outer space, whether carried out by government or non-governmental entities. Therefore, Irish neutrality could be compromised through private sector entanglement in military-capable space infrastructure unless stricter national legislation is introduced to safeguard against dual-use participation.

The United Kingdom's exit from the European union has forced Ireland into a complex rebalancing act. While Brexit is largely viewed as a trade and sovereignty issue, it has profound implications for Ireland's geopolitical and defence posture.

With Britain no longer part of the EU, Ireland has become the Union's primary English-speaking member and the only one with a direct land border with the UK. This places Ireland in a sensitive position: politically closer to the EU but geographically tied to a neighbour with a divergent security policy—one increasingly aligned with the United States and NATO.

This divergence places pressure on Ireland to harmonize more closely with EU Common Security and Defence Policy (CSDP) initiatives, particularly under PESCO. Though Ireland participates in "non-lethal" projects, Brexit has weakened the informal alliance of smaller, non-aligned EU states that previously buffered Irish reluctance toward military integration.

Furthermore, UK–Ireland bilateral security arrangements, such as the air defence pact, now operate outside the EU framework. In times of geopolitical tension, this creates ambiguity: who would coordinate airspace defence over Ireland if the UK were engaged in a conflict from which Ireland abstains?

Brexit has no direct legal bearing on Ireland's neutrality, but it alters the treaty landscape. Ireland remains subject to Article 42.7 of the Treaty on European Union, which includes a mutual defence clause. Though Ireland has a neutrality clause in its national policy, it has not enshrined neutrality constitutionally. Without constitutional protection, future governments may interpret EU defence clauses in ways that incrementally erode Ireland's non-aligned status. This chapter ties closely to **Chapter 9: Ireland, NATO and the EU** for extended legal analysis.

Neutrality is not a shield against climate-induced geopolitical stress. Climate change is rapidly becoming a threat multiplier, amplifying global conflicts over water, food, migration, and habitable land. For Ireland, the challenge is twofold: direct exposure to extreme weather events and indirect pressure from global instability.

Rising sea levels threaten Irish coastal communities, but more broadly, climate disruption may produce massive migration from vulnerable regions. As a member of the EU, Ireland will be drawn into debates over climate refugees, border control, and humanitarian aid—issues that blur the line between civil policy and strategic response.

Moreover, the militaries of major powers are reconfiguring for climate conflict—building Arctic bases, securing freshwater resources, and training for mass-displacement scenarios. Ireland, as a neutral nation, must decide whether it can remain outside such strategic planning, especially if climate migration routes pass through or near its territory.

Irish peacekeeping missions may also be increasingly deployed to climate-affected zones under UN or EU mandates. This raises questions about the neutrality of participating in missions driven by resource conflict or environmental collapse.

International law does not yet define environmental disruption as a trigger for armed conflict or self-defence under the UN Charter. However, the Geneva Conventions and related protocols do prohibit warfare that causes "widespread, long-term and severe damage to the natural environment." Ireland could play a unique legal role in advocating for a new environmental neutrality doctrine—protecting neutral nations from being drawn into climate-related security operations. Until such a framework is established, ambiguity remains, and collective EU responses to climate crises could override neutrality.

While not an Arctic nation, Ireland's proximity to the North Atlantic makes it an indirect stakeholder in the unfolding contest over the Arctic. Melting ice has opened new shipping routes, accelerated resource exploration, and triggered a scramble for influence among Russia, China, the U.S., and NATO.

Iceland, Norway, and Denmark—all militarily aligned states—are ramping up Arctic patrols. Ireland, by contrast, has no Arctic presence, no ice-capable vessels, and no legal claim under the Arctic Council framework. Yet as routes shift closer to Irish maritime zones, and with potential offshore energy claims expanding northward, Ireland will inevitably be pulled into Arctic geopolitics.

The Arctic is also becoming a theatre for militarized satellite deployment and long-range missile testing. As noted in **Section 5.3**, this raises major concerns for neutral states. Ireland's data cables, ports, and air routes may become logistical nodes in Arctic-adjacent operations, regardless of policy preferences.

Economically, Irish shipping and fisheries may benefit from Arctic trade, but these gains come with geopolitical entanglement. If Ireland cooperates with Arctic surveillance or emergency response missions—especially under EU or NATO frameworks—it risks undermining its neutral status.

The Arctic Council's legal framework does not bind Ireland but must still observe the Law of the Sea and environmental treaties related to polar activity. As a non-Arctic state, any future military or surveillance activity must be scrutinized under Ireland's neutrality principles. If Ireland permits use of its territory or airspace in support of Arctic militarization, even indirectly, it risks violating the Hague Conventions and compromising its position as a neutral party. Proactive legislative safeguards may be required to prevent covert alignment.

3

CYBERSECURITY AND HYBRID WARFARE

Neutral countries are increasingly targeted in cyberspace, not because they are belligerents, but precisely because they are perceived as under-defended and geopolitically non-aligned. Cyber warfare provides a potent tool for adversaries to exert influence or gather intelligence without the visible footprint of traditional military aggression. For neutral states, this creates a dangerous paradox: their very neutrality makes them more likely to be treated as soft targets in a conflict that doesn't follow conventional rules of war.

These threats are not speculative—they are actively being deployed. Cyberattacks now include espionage campaigns, ransomware strikes, denial-of-service incidents, infrastructure sabotage, and widespread data theft. The goal is not always immediate disruption, but long-term degradation of a state's ability to govern or assert its sovereignty. This makes countries such as Ireland, with sensitive data centres, submarine cables, cloud services, and legal jurisdictions attractive for multinational operations, uniquely vulnerable.

The distributed and anonymized nature of cyber operations compounds this threat. Unlike conventional invasions, cyber incursions can be launched from anywhere, routed through third-party infrastructure, and executed without attribution. This limits a neutral state's ability to respond diplomatically, legally, or even detect such intrusions before significant damage has occurred.

Under international law, this evolving threat space poses major problems. Article 2(4) of the UN Charter prohibits the use of force, but whether a cyberattack constitutes "force" is often debated. The Tallinn Manual, while influential, is non-binding and fails to compel states to respond to grey-area intrusions. Even where cyberattacks cause systemic disruption, if they don't result in direct injury or destruction, they often fall short of the threshold for legal self-defence under Article 51. Neutral states, therefore, face an unenforceable legal vacuum unless new treaty instruments or domestic doctrines are created to define and defend a concept of cyber neutrality.

Ireland's exposure is uniquely acute due to its status as a digital hub for Europe. With many of the world's largest tech companies headquartered in Dublin, Ireland's digital assets and infrastructure attract the attention of state-sponsored hackers and rogue networks alike. However, its legal neutrality has not been extended to the digital sphere, leaving Ireland straddling a dangerous fault line between its geopolitical stance and its economic dependencies.

The national cybersecurity framework, while improving, remains underdeveloped. Ireland currently lacks a formal military cyber command, and the civilian-run National Cyber Security Centre (NCSC) is often under-resourced and politically constrained. Much of Ireland's cybersecurity posture is thus reliant on either private-sector providers or EU-level cooperation—neither of which can act decisively or independently in times of crisis. This erodes sovereign control and weakens response coherence.

Ireland's deep integration with both EU and U.S. digital ecosystems adds another layer of vulnerability. In the event of geopolitical tension between major powers, Ireland could find itself a proxy battleground, targeted not for its own political decisions but because its servers and cables are instrumental to others. There is also a policy and legislative gap in how Ireland handles sensitive assets such as encrypted data, cloud servers, and financial technologies. These digital assets are critical to modern sovereignty but enjoy none of the protections afforded to traditional security sectors.

The Cybercrime Act 2017 focuses primarily on criminal behaviour but provides no doctrinal foundation for handling state-level threats or establishing digital neutrality. Furthermore, Ireland's participation in certain EU cybersecurity and defence programmes may compromise its appearance of neutrality, even if unintended. The absence of a constitutional or strategic doctrine addressing cyberspace leaves Ireland vulnerable both in practice and in perception.

The global record of cyberattacks on neutral nations is a warning to Ireland. Finland and Sweden, prior to NATO accession, were subjected to frequent attacks attributed to Russian state-backed groups. These included coordinated disinformation campaigns, digital interference in democratic processes, and attacks on energy infrastructure—all aimed at political destabilisation without overt military force. These cyber campaigns helped shift the public debate in both countries towards alliance with NATO.

Switzerland, another longstanding neutral, has also been repeatedly targeted. Cyber-espionage operations have focused on financial institutions and diplomatic correspondence, exploiting the trust placed in Swiss discretion and the assumption that Swiss systems would not retaliate or call for international intervention.

Austria provides an equally stark example. In 2019, its Foreign Ministry was hit with a sophisticated cyberattack attributed to a state actor. Despite its neutrality, Austria's EU ties and intelligence-sharing roles made it a valuable target. The attackers were able to penetrate sensitive servers without any form of traditional violation of sovereignty.

Even Ireland has not been spared. In 2021, the Health Service Executive was paralysed by a ransomware attack reportedly linked to Russian-speaking cybercriminals. Though not officially classified as an act of war, the attack had the hallmarks of a strategic campaign—disrupting public services, shaking public trust, and demonstrating Ireland's institutional vulnerability.

These examples underscore that neutrality, in its current form, provides no meaningful protection against cyber threats. Legal protections rooted in 20th-century treaties fail to address the reality of 21st-century digital coercion. UN Resolution 73/27 affirmed that international law applies in cyberspace, but it lacks enforcement mechanisms, leaving neutral states in a reactive and isolated position.

To defend itself in the evolving battlespace of hybrid conflict, Ireland must articulate a clear, enforceable cyber-neutrality doctrine. This strategy cannot rest solely on technical upgrades or vague political declarations; it must be anchored in law, diplomacy, infrastructure, and institutional capacity.

A starting point is the legal definition of cyber neutrality itself. Ireland must formally define its role as a digitally neutral actor in national legislation, setting out protocols for foreign cyber incursions, thresholds for response, and guidelines for infrastructure protection. This definition should draw on international examples such as the Tallinn Manual but be embedded in binding domestic law.

The existing National Cyber Security Centre should be expanded and reconstituted as a national cyber defence agency. This agency would be tasked with coordinating cybersecurity efforts across all sectors—public and private—including counterintelligence, digital diplomacy, and incident response. It would need statutory independence, a mandate beyond simple technical compliance, and the ability to act in times of geopolitical escalation.

Ireland could also lead internationally by proposing a Digital Geneva Initiative—an effort at the UN or EU level to codify the rights and protections of civilian digital infrastructure in neutral states. In parallel, a Critical Infrastructure Security Framework should be developed to audit and regulate digital vulnerabilities across energy, healthcare, transport, finance, and communication sectors. This framework must include enforceable regulations that require sovereign control over vital cybersecurity measures, including physical hosting and encryption standards.

Ireland should initiate a Global Non-Alignment Charter for Cyberspace, forming a coalition with other neutral or non-aligned states such as Switzerland, Austria, and Singapore. This coalition would jointly assert the rights of neutral states against coercive digital practices and build reciprocal intelligence-sharing and crisis-response protocols outside of military blocs such as NATO.

These reforms must be legally integrated into existing obligations under instruments like the Budapest Convention on Cybercrime and the EU's NIS2 Directive. Crucially, domestic legislation must be updated to ensure that cooperation with foreign powers or participation in external programmes does not inadvertently breach Ireland's neutrality. Without constitutional recognition of cyber neutrality, these reforms risk being undermined by future governments under pressure from allies or adversaries alike.

Hybrid warfare operates in the murky territory between diplomacy and open conflict, designed specifically to exploit legal ambiguity and political hesitation. Rather than deploying tanks and fighter jets, hybrid attacks blend digital sabotage, disinformation, financial manipulation, economic blackmail, and civil disruption to degrade a state's sovereignty without triggering formal war powers or international interventions. For neutral nations like Ireland, this evolving mode of aggression presents a complex and highly asymmetric challenge.

Historically, Irish neutrality was predicated on a clear divide between war and peace, between allies and adversaries. Hybrid warfare subverts this binary. It does not depend on formal declarations or physical invasions. Instead, it erodes a state's stability through low-visibility, deniable methods. In this new arena, Ireland's openness—digital, economic, and political—becomes a potential liability. The country's limited military expenditure, open data architecture, and reliance on foreign-owned platforms create exploitable vectors for manipulation. Moreover, Ireland's status as Europe's primary tech hub makes it a proxy target for larger global tensions.

Tactics associated with hybrid operations include covert influence in domestic media, the manipulation of supply chains, data theft or ransom targeting key public institutions, and foreign-backed disinformation aimed at polarising society. These methods bypass the traditional protections afforded by neutrality and strike directly at democratic systems and civil trust. Because hybrid operations often unfold below the legal threshold of war, they frequently go unpunished, encouraging further abuse.

In the legal domain, hybrid warfare exists largely in a grey zone. Although Article 2(4) of the UN Charter prohibits the use of force, and the Rome Statute outlines crimes during conflict, neither clearly defines the subversive acts that constitute hybrid aggression. Psychological warfare, financial destabilisation, and cyber sabotage are rarely addressed as actionable violations under existing frameworks. This ambiguity allows powerful actors to operate with impunity, leaving small, neutral states vulnerable and diplomatically paralysed.

The risk is not theoretical. The playbook of hybrid warfare has been field-tested on a range of neutral and non-aligned countries. Estonia's experience in 2007 was one of the first internationally recognised hybrid campaigns. Following a dispute over the relocation of a Soviet monument, the country suffered sustained cyberattacks on its banking, government, and media infrastructure—crippling public systems and demonstrating how digital aggression could yield political results without firing a shot. At the time, NATO struggled to determine whether Article 5 could be invoked, exposing gaps in collective defence models when responding to non-kinetic threats.

Ukraine, before Russia's 2014 annexation of Crimea, was subject to prolonged hybrid destabilisation. Cyberattacks, gas pipeline interference, currency manipulation, and orchestrated disinformation campaigns steadily eroded national stability and divided public opinion, softening resistance ahead of military incursions. These tactics—incremental, layered, and ambiguous—are now standard in the hybrid warfare arsenal.

Even Finland, before joining NATO, experienced pressure via hybrid means. These included cyber incursions, energy dependency exploitation, and carefully timed migration pressure along borders—each calibrated to challenge national resilience and probe political red lines without triggering open conflict.

In Ireland's case, the 2021 ransomware attack on the Health Service Executive revealed how hybrid tools can disable vital infrastructure while falling short of conventional aggression. Though believed to be carried out by criminal groups, the scale and impact of the attack suggested sophistication and coordination of a type often linked to state actors. The disruption to healthcare services demonstrated how unarmed, digital coercion can achieve strategic disruption traditionally associated with wartime sabotage.

Such examples confirm that hybrid warfare is already shaping geopolitical contests, and Ireland—by virtue of its digital infrastructure, neutrality, and economic openness—is a frontline target.

Ireland's response to these threats cannot be reactive. It must be strategic, pre-emptive, and grounded in constitutional and legal clarity. A cornerstone of this strategy should be the creation of a National Hybrid Warfare Response Unit (NHWRU). This agency, formed by statute and reporting to the Oireachtas, would be tasked with the identification, classification, and response to hybrid threats—including cyberattacks, foreign disinformation, psychological operations, and economic coercion.

The NHWRU would operate independently but coordinate with the National Cyber Security Centre, Defence Forces, and Department of Foreign Affairs. It would consist of a multidisciplinary team incorporating cyber analysts, constitutional lawyers, psychological operations specialists, and forensic intelligence officers. Its mandate would extend to real-time monitoring of digital and media threats, rapid policy intervention, and legal response coordination. Unlike existing institutions, it would not be constrained by bureaucratic silos, but structured to operate flexibly in the face of fluid, asymmetric attacks.

Legally, this unit would require a clear statutory foundation, including defined thresholds for when hybrid attacks rise to the level of national security threats. It would also need legal mechanisms to propose emergency legislation, monitor foreign investments or partnerships that risk undermining neutrality, and prepare yearly reports for parliamentary review. To ensure transparency and accountability, it should be subject to oversight by a cross-party committee and supervised by an independent ombudsman focused on digital and civil rights.

Ireland's future neutrality depends not on detachment, but on determined, intelligent engagement with the threats of the modern world. This means first recognising that hybrid warfare poses an existential challenge that cannot be met by military abstention alone. Neutrality today must be proactive, not passive.

To begin, Ireland must introduce a constitutional or statutory recognition of hybrid aggression as a distinct category of national security threat. This would bridge the legal gap between crime and war, enabling a calibrated, lawful response to incidents that fall short of kinetic force but undermine sovereignty. Such a reform aligns with proposals detailed in **Chapter 14: The Irish Neutrality and Sovereignty Act,** and is essential for avoiding ad hoc or politically improvised responses in moments of crisis.

Secondly, Ireland should lead the development of a digital neutrality doctrine, one that reimagines the principles of non-alignment for the cyber age. This doctrine would guide legislation, bilateral agreements, infrastructure development, and international alliances. It would make clear that Ireland's neutrality includes the defence of its networks, data, institutions, and civic stability against any form of covert aggression.

Internationally, Ireland must establish new alliances grounded in digital and hybrid resilience. Rather than aligning with NATO or PESCO, it should collaborate with similarly positioned neutral nations—such as Switzerland, Austria, and Singapore—to form a Digital Non-Alignment Pact. This agreement could facilitate intelligence-sharing, develop joint crisis protocols, and create common definitions of hostile digital acts. It would also reinforce Ireland's commitment to peaceful internationalism while building tangible protection against 21st-century coercion.

Ireland's critical infrastructure—from power grids and water systems to hospitals and transport networks—must undergo a national resilience audit. Following this, legislation should be enacted to ensure that these systems meet cybersecurity benchmarks, are locally managed or encrypted, and have redundancy protocols. These physical protections are the corollary of digital sovereignty and are fundamental to withstanding hybrid assault.

A final, and perhaps most important pillar of defence, is civic resilience. Ireland must invest in a national cognitive security initiative aimed at making the public resistant to disinformation, foreign agitation, and social polarisation. Public broadcasting, independent journalism, and educational reform should all play a role in reinforcing democratic literacy and media awareness. No state can withstand hybrid aggression if its population is easily manipulated or divided.

To oversee these reforms, the government should establish a Neutrality Enforcement Office within the Department of the Taoiseach or Attorney General's Office. This office would assess all government actions—including international agreements, procurement deals, and digital infrastructure plans—for compliance with Ireland's neutrality doctrine.

In sum, neutrality in the age of hybrid warfare is not about stepping back—it is about standing firm. It requires Ireland to adopt a legally fortified, technologically resilient, and diplomatically principled stance against an adversary that will never declare war but will always test weakness. If this roadmap is followed, Ireland can not only preserve its neutrality, but redefine it as a model of civilian-based, rights-protecting, 21st-century security.

4

WHAT IS THE TRIPLE LOCK

If Irish neutrality is the principle, then the Triple Lock is its most tangible constitutional safeguard—an institutional firewall built to prevent unmandated military entanglement. It is not simply a procedural hurdle; it is a democratic expression of sovereignty. The Triple Lock ensures that decisions to deploy Irish forces into international conflict zones are filtered through not one, but three separate layers of accountability: international legality, executive discretion, and parliamentary oversight.

The term "Triple Lock" may suggest a technicality, but its foundation is philosophical. It recognizes that no single entity—whether it be the United Nations, the Irish Cabinet, or the Dáil Éireann—should possess unilateral power to send Irish soldiers into battle. It requires all three to agree. The result is a compound system of restraint: if one lock fails, the door remains closed. This model is rare in global governance, and rarer still in states with advanced military capabilities. For Ireland, it is a signal to the world—and to itself—that military deployment is an exceptional act, not a default policy.

At its core, the Triple Lock rests on three pillars. First, there must be an explicit mandate from the United Nations, usually through a Security Council resolution. This requirement is not a mere formality; it places Irish military action within the framework of international law, ensuring that any engagement is multilaterally sanctioned and legally grounded. Second, the Irish Government must endorse the deployment, affirming that the proposed mission aligns with the nation's values, strategic interests, and foreign policy. Third, and most importantly from a democratic standpoint, the Dáil must approve the action, granting the elected representatives of the Irish people a final say in whether the Republic crosses the line from peacekeeping to participation in armed conflict.

This process does not simply delay military decisions—it de-escalates them. By requiring a triple confirmation, the mechanism injects time, scrutiny, and political debate into moments that, elsewhere, may be governed by executive haste or alliance pressure. It deliberately slows down the machinery of war.

To understand its origins, one must revisit the early 2000s—a time of geopolitical turbulence in the aftermath of the 9/11 attacks and the invasions of Afghanistan and Iraq. Ireland, though militarily modest, was exposed to growing calls for alignment with U.S. and NATO interests. The specter of mission creep into foreign theaters—especially through ambiguous support roles like airspace use or logistical aid—prompted a reckoning. There was rising discomfort among citizens and politicians alike that Ireland might be sleepwalking into foreign wars under the guise of partnership.

The introduction of the Triple Lock was a preemptive assertion of moral independence. It was a response to the unease that Ireland's neutrality could be undermined not through declaration, but through quiet cooperation and creeping obligation. The Triple Lock was created to define the threshold clearly and constitutionally. If Ireland was to fight, it would do so only with international legitimacy, national interest, and democratic approval—not on the strength of political pressure or ideological fashion.

It is a system designed for complexity. In an age where military missions are increasingly hybrid—combining humanitarian relief with combat readiness, counter-terrorism with capacity-building—the Triple Lock offers clarity. It filters out operations that blur the line between peacekeeping and warfare. It enables Ireland to send soldiers abroad in support of peace, but only when the mission is unambiguously lawful, proportionate, and endorsed by the people's representatives.

Yet the very strength of the Triple Lock is also the source of its political friction. Some critics describe it as "too restrictive," arguing that it hobbles Ireland's ability to respond swiftly to evolving threats. Others say it creates a dependency on the whims of the UN Security Council, where permanent members can veto action for reasons of their own national interest, not global justice. Within the European Union, some policymakers have quietly suggested that Ireland's refusal to streamline military integration into EU defense structures is an impediment to "strategic autonomy."

But this critique misses the point. The Triple Lock was never intended to be nimble. It was designed to be cautious. It is a democratic speed bump, not a bureaucratic wall. It is meant to provoke pause and demand consensus—something far too rare in international security affairs.

The stakes are not hypothetical. Ireland's refusal to join the U.S.-led invasion of Iraq in 2003 is one of the clearest illustrations of the Triple Lock in action. Despite diplomatic pressure and ideological fervor, Ireland did not follow the path of many Western allies. There was no UN resolution authorizing the invasion. The Dáil was not convinced. And so, the locks held. While the government controversially allowed U.S. military aircraft to refuel at Shannon Airport, the symbolic and operational refusal to enter the war as a combatant remained intact. This was not a matter of convenience—it was constitutional principle in motion.

Yet the continued use of Shannon Airport by U.S. military forces remains a flashpoint. Critics argue that allowing military aircraft to land on Irish soil, even without deploying Irish troops, is a violation of neutrality in spirit, if not in law. These tensions underscore a deeper issue: even with the Triple Lock in place, neutrality must be constantly defended against erosion, not just from outside powers but from within—by successive governments tempted to bypass public scrutiny in the name of expediency or alliance management.

As calls grow louder to abandon or amend the Triple Lock—framed as "reform" by some and "dismantlement" by others—it becomes imperative to ask: who benefits from removing this safeguard? What would Ireland become without it? Would a weakened or removed Triple Lock render Ireland more secure, or merely more pliable to the interests of larger powers?

The answers are not abstract. They lie in the recent history of global conflict, where small states that tethered their fate to larger alliances found themselves drawn into wars they neither initiated nor benefited from. They lie in the public consciousness of a nation that, time and again, has affirmed its desire to remain neutral—not because it fears war, but because it dares to imagine peace as an act of strength.

The Triple Lock mechanism, although politically powerful, exists as a policy framework rather than constitutional law. Its three components—UN authorization, Government approval, and Dáil approval—do not appear in a single legal instrument but are embedded in administrative practice and parliamentary convention, including ministerial responsibilities under the Defence Acts and Government Orders for overseas deployment. Legally, this construct has helped align Ireland with international law standards, particularly Article 51 of the UN Charter (self-defense) and Chapter VI and VII mandates for peace enforcement. However, because the Triple Lock is not enshrined in the Constitution or primary legislation, it remains vulnerable to reinterpretation or abolition by a simple majority vote in the Oireachtas. If dismantled without a public mandate or constitutional amendment, the Irish Government could face domestic judicial review and international reputational damage. Participation in military operations without UN approval may constitute a breach of the UN Charter, and military deployment without lawful justification could render Irish officials individually liable under the Rome Statute for aiding or abetting crimes of aggression or breaches of jus cogens (compelling norms of international law). Therefore, the legal architecture underpinning the Triple Lock, while symbolically robust, is legally fragile, and its dismantling would likely require a national referendum to align with constitutional principles of democratic legitimacy.

Beyond legal structure, the Triple Lock functions as a civic instrument designed to decentralize war-making power. It reflects a commitment to participatory democracy by embedding public values—peace, restraint, accountability—into the process of military engagement. In contrast to executive-led military powers in larger nations, the Triple Lock affirms that foreign military action requires not just technical legality, but moral legitimacy and democratic consent. This structure also promotes public trust. When people see their elected representatives empowered to debate and vote on military matters, they are more likely to see national security as something owned by citizens, not dictated by elites. Moreover, the system aligns with Irish political culture, which favors consensus over coercion and consultation over command—a vital distinction in safeguarding both neutrality and public confidence in state integrity.

5

HOW THE TRIPLE LOCK WORKS IN PRACTICE

Understanding the Triple Lock requires more than dissecting legal clauses or interpreting constitutional language. It requires examining how it functions—or fails—in moments of pressure, in real geopolitical events, and under the weight of competing interests. As discussed in **Chapter 4**, the Triple Lock is a layered decision-making framework: UN authorization, Irish Government assent, and Dáil Éireann approval. But its meaning is fully revealed not in theory, but in action.

One of the clearest demonstrations of the Triple Lock functioning as intended is Ireland's role in United Nations peacekeeping missions. Consider the long-standing deployment to Lebanon under the United Nations Interim Force in Lebanon (UNIFIL). Initiated in 1978, this mission exemplifies how all three components of the Triple Lock converge to legitimate Irish involvement abroad. UNIFIL was and remains a mission with clear UN backing, consistent with the UN Charter, aimed at stabilizing a volatile border region between Lebanon and Israel.

Here, the government assessed the mission's alignment with Irish values—non-aggression, humanitarian support, and the promotion of peace. The Dáil ratified that involvement, reflecting widespread political and public support. Through this process, Ireland sent troops not to intervene in war, but to act as neutral peacekeepers in a multilateral, internationally mandated effort. That distinction is not semantic—it is the lifeblood of how Ireland distinguishes itself on the global stage.

This mission, like others in Congo, Liberia, Mali, and East Timor, has demonstrated the kind of foreign policy that Irish neutrality enables: active, moral, and effective without being militarized. These are not deployments driven by imperial allegiance or regional blocs; they are grounded in legal legitimacy and democratic accountability. Each one stands as proof that neutrality does not mean isolation—it means discernment.

Yet contrast this with the case of Shannon Airport, touched on in **Chapter 4**. During the U.S.-led invasion of Iraq in 2003, Ireland's airspace and territory became a waypoint for American military aircraft, despite the fact that Ireland itself did not participate in the war. The government at the time argued this was a logistical allowance, not military cooperation. But that rationale fell flat with much of the public and several legal scholars, who saw it as a bypass of the spirit—if not the technical wording—of neutrality.

The Triple Lock was not engaged because no Irish troops were sent. But this loophole became a litmus test for the government's commitment to neutrality. If the locks apply only to direct deployment, then logistical support for foreign wars—even those condemned internationally—could occur without triggering democratic or legal scrutiny. The result was an erosion of public trust in the robustness of neutrality protections.

The Shannon controversy lingers not only because of the war it supported, but because it revealed a vulnerability in the interpretation of the Triple Lock itself. If military engagement is narrowly defined as boots on the ground, then a host of activities—refueling, intelligence sharing, overflights—remain in the grey zone. It is precisely this ambiguity that critics of recent "defense reforms" fear. Without expanding or clarifying the legal understanding of the Triple Lock, governments can technically comply while morally drifting away from neutrality.

The government's role in this is pivotal. It holds the power to propose deployments, manage foreign policy, and interpret legal provisions surrounding international cooperation. In recent years, statements from high-ranking officials have suggested a desire to "modernize" Ireland's defense posture, including potential adjustments to the Triple Lock. In March 2025, the Tánaiste remarked that Ireland is in a "serious period of reform" regarding security and defense—a phrase that, to some, signals the beginning of a strategic pivot toward deeper integration with EU and NATO frameworks.

While such statements are often presented in the language of pragmatism, they are anything but neutral. They imply that the current system—one of rigorous democratic checks and multilateral consensus—is outdated. But as detailed previously, the Triple Lock is not an accidental legacy of the early 2000s; it is a response to genuine risks. It exists not to stall Ireland's relevance, but to preserve its integrity.

There have been quieter examples of the Triple Lock in action that are less public but no less instructive. Ireland's participation in EU Battlegroups, for instance, has tested the boundaries of neutrality without overtly violating the Lock. These groups are rapid response units composed of multinational EU forces, designed to deploy in crisis zones under short notice. While their stated purposes are often humanitarian or stabilizing, the speed and opacity of their operations raise concerns. In most cases, Ireland's involvement has been limited to planning or training. However, any attempt to deploy Irish troops under such a banner would still require Triple Lock approval. So far, this has acted as a brake, not a break, in Ireland's policy of military restraint.

The United Nations remains the keystone of the first lock. Its legitimacy grants Ireland the moral and legal foundation to participate in missions without violating neutrality. But this dependency is also a vulnerability. As permanent members of the UN Security Council wield veto power, multilateral missions can be blocked for reasons unrelated to justice or humanitarian need. If Ireland wishes to deploy forces on a peacekeeping mission that is stalled in the Security Council, the Triple Lock can halt the effort—even if the mission is broadly supported globally.

This paradox illustrates both the strength and the limits of the system. It demands consensus even when consensus is politically difficult. But rather than weaken the Triple Lock for the sake of convenience, this challenge argues for more innovative diplomacy: using Ireland's international credibility to rally broader support for Security Council reform, or to build partnerships that work within its legal boundaries.

Ultimately, the practical application of the Triple Lock is a test of values versus pressures. It is easy to uphold neutrality in times of calm. It is far more difficult when allies call for solidarity, when economic partners demand cooperation, or when crises unfold at pace. But it is precisely in those moments that the mechanism proves its worth. The Triple Lock is not a tool of indecision; it is a declaration that Ireland will not be stampeded into war, no matter how urgent the headlines.

To defend the Triple Lock in practice is to engage constantly with its interpretation. It requires oversight, vigilance, and education. It demands that governments be held to account when they attempt to circumvent its intent. And it asks citizens to recognize that neutrality is not passive, but participatory—that true neutrality is earned, not assumed.

The legal issues related to the operational use of the Triple Lock, particularly in the context of UN peacekeeping missions, have generally adhered to both international law and Ireland's stated policy of neutrality. Missions such as UNIFIL (Lebanon) or MONUC (Congo) were conducted under clear UN Security Council resolutions and with full parliamentary oversight. These engagements meet the criteria for lawful use of force under Chapter VII of the UN Charter, providing international legitimacy and legal immunity for Irish soldiers operating under UN command. However, the Shannon Airport precedent, as previously mentioned, exposes Ireland to legal vulnerability. Despite not deploying troops, allowing the use of sovereign territory for logistics in wars lacking UN approval could violate the laws of neutrality under customary international law and Hague Convention V. Moreover, if weapons or military personnel transported through Shannon were later involved in violations of the Geneva Conventions, Ireland could be seen as facilitating or enabling war crimes, especially under Articles 25 and 28 of the Rome Statute, which address complicity and command responsibility. No formal legal mechanism currently subjects such decisions (e.g., refueling permissions) to the Triple Lock, creating a legal loophole in a system otherwise built on multilayered consent. This gap may warrant a judicial review or legislative amendment to bring Shannon operations into alignment with Ireland's stated obligations under international and humanitarian law.

Ireland's global reputation for peacekeeping has become part of its soft power identity, cultivated not through defense pacts but through consistent neutrality and visible humanitarian engagement. Missions like those in Lebanon, Congo, and Mali are not just foreign policy actions—they are moral statements. These deployments have built an image of Ireland as a nation that shows up not to conquer, but to calm, acting in solidarity with communities in crisis. Importantly, this peacekeeping role also reinforces the functionality of the Triple Lock by demonstrating that military capability and neutrality are not mutually exclusive. Irish troops carry not just weapons, but trust—particularly in post-colonial or politically fractured zones where aligned forces are viewed with suspicion. This strategic neutrality enhances Ireland's international credibility, positioning the state as a non-threatening, values-driven actor capable of bridging divides where others bring division.

6

THE IRISH NEUTRALITY MOVEMENT

The Irish neutrality movement is not a relic of Cold War politics nor a fringe resistance to modernity—it is an evolving civic force rooted in the belief that peace is a strategic and moral choice. It is both a defensive line against external pressures and an internal call to preserve a distinct national identity. Unlike many other countries where defense policy is the domain of generals and technocrats, in Ireland, neutrality lives in the public square, voiced by poets, peacekeepers, academics, students, farmers, and veterans alike.

As detailed in **Chapter 5**, neutrality is safeguarded in policy terms by the Triple Lock. But a mechanism is only as resilient as the will to defend it. That will is found in the neutrality movement—a broad coalition of citizens, civil society organizations, and political actors who view neutrality not just as a position, but as a principle that must be renewed through constant participation and cultural engagement.

The threats to neutrality are not imagined. Ireland's increasing involvement in EU security structures, its accommodation of foreign military aircraft through Shannon Airport, and the government's expressed desire to review defense policy have created a sense of urgency within the movement. The concern is not only that neutrality might be abandoned in a single, dramatic act—but that it may be eroded quietly, by degrees, until it becomes symbolic rather than substantive.

The neutrality movement is therefore as much about awareness as it is about action. It begins with a simple assertion: neutrality is not outdated. It is, in fact, more relevant than ever in an era of endless proxy wars, artificial intelligence in warfare, and global security blocs that often act in their own interest rather than the collective good. Irish neutrality offers a vision of foreign policy that is democratic, independent, and ethical—a counterbalance to the normalization of militarism in international affairs.

This movement is also increasingly conscious of its global dimension. Ireland is not alone in its stance. Countries like Switzerland and Austria maintain similar positions, even as they face analogous pressures from neighboring powers and collective defense treaties. The idea of a neutral bloc—cooperating on humanitarian, environmental, and diplomatic issues while remaining militarily non-aligned—is gaining traction. Irish neutrality, therefore, is not a stance of isolation, but a node in a wider network of nations that seek alternative approaches to security and influence.

But this vision will not survive on ideals alone. The movement understands that education is its greatest weapon. Schools, universities, libraries, and local organizations have become battlegrounds in the effort to educate new generations on what neutrality means, why it was chosen, and what it has allowed Ireland to become on the world stage. The goal is not merely historical remembrance, but civic renewal. Young people are urged not just to inherit neutrality, but to interrogate it, defend it, and evolve it.

This is why the neutrality movement is inherently grassroots. It is bottom-up, not top-down. It thrives in communities, online platforms, independent media, and public lectures. It is found in protest marches outside Shannon, in poetry readings commemorating peacekeeping missions, and in neighborhood forums discussing Ireland's place in a dangerous world. These aren't acts of nostalgia—they are expressions of vigilance. In them, neutrality is kept alive not as dogma, but as civic choice.

The movement also resists being co-opted by political polarization. It draws strength from the fact that neutrality, as a value, crosses party lines. It is not a leftist ideal nor a conservative stronghold. It appeals to people who value sovereignty, those who fear imperial overreach, those who believe in non-violence, and those who reject the logic of permanent warfare. This pluralism makes the movement resilient, but it also means it must constantly articulate a unifying vision. That vision, at its core, is the belief that Ireland can best serve humanity by refusing to serve any war machine.

In parallel, cultural activism plays a powerful role. Neutrality is woven into Ireland's artistic identity: in songs that remember peacekeepers lost in distant lands; in films that contrast neutrality with the tragedies of interventionism; in murals that frame Irish history as a story of resistance to domination, not just foreign but ideological. These cultural expressions make neutrality tangible, emotional, and personal. They move the debate out of parliamentary chambers and into the imagination of the people.

Still, the neutrality movement does not operate under illusions. It acknowledges the world has changed. Cyberattacks, asymmetric warfare, and supranational security deals present new challenges to an old doctrine. But the movement's strength lies not in denying complexity, but in asserting that neutrality can adapt without being abandoned. It advocates for new models of cybersecurity, for enhanced diplomatic training, for peace-oriented international partnerships. It offers vision, not just resistance.

To do this, the movement must remain organized. Local action groups, national campaigns, and international solidarity networks are key to resisting efforts to quietly normalize military alignment. Coordination with legal experts, scholars, and international watchdogs helps expose policy shifts that might otherwise pass unnoticed. The movement doesn't merely protest; it scrutinizes draft legislation, issues policy briefs, engages with media, and initiates legal challenges when required. It is activism with a backbone.

Young people are central to this work. Ireland's neutrality movement has, over the past decade, grown visibly more youthful—partly because of education efforts, and partly because the youth sense what is at stake. They see neutrality not as parochial self-protection but as a progressive stand against the militarization of everything: politics, policing, technology, and even borders. In their eyes, neutrality aligns with environmentalism, international solidarity, and digital freedom. This is a powerful alliance of causes—one the movement increasingly embraces.

Digital tools have amplified this reach. Social media campaigns, podcasts, interactive infographics, and digital storytelling now allow the movement to connect across generations and borders. Campaigns like #NeutralIreland or #KeepIrelandOut have emerged as modern rallying cries. In these digital spaces, neutrality is no longer an obscure policy; it is a trend, a lifestyle, a statement.

Yet the movement's greatest strength may lie in its moral clarity. While others argue for alignment in the name of practicality, the neutrality movement argues for independence in the name of principle. It maintains that no country, especially one as small and historically colonized as Ireland, should delegate its defense or foreign policy decisions to any superpower or supranational bloc. It believes Ireland's credibility comes not from its alliances, but from its honesty. And it insists that peace is not weakness—it is wisdom.

Neutrality will not survive by accident. It must be fought for, campaigned for, and reimagined. The neutrality movement is not asking Ireland to retreat from the world—it is demanding that Ireland lead by example, as it has done in peacekeeping, in diplomacy, and in the global fight for justice.

The next chapter explores the pressure points applied by larger actors—namely NATO—and the mythology surrounding Ireland's so-called security deficits. But before examining those external forces, it is worth remembering: the most effective defender of neutrality is not a treaty or a constitutional clause—it is the will of the people.

The Irish neutrality movement, while primarily civic in nature, operates within a complex and sometimes precarious legal environment. Activists exercising their rights to protest, assemble, and express dissent are protected under both Irish constitutional law and international human rights law. Article 40.6.1 of Bunreacht na hÉireann protects freedom of speech, peaceful assembly, and association, while the European Convention on Human Rights (ECHR)—incorporated into Irish law through the European Convention on Human Rights Act 2003—guarantees the rights to protest and free expression under Articles 10 and 11. These protections extend to online activities such as organizing, publishing opinions, and critiquing defense policy or government actions perceived to erode neutrality.

However, legal tensions emerge in specific areas. Peaceful protests at locations like Shannon Airport, for example, have frequently resulted in arrests and prosecutions under the Criminal Damage Act 1991, Public Order

Acts, and Trespass legislation, often invoking concerns about national security, public safety, or interference with critical infrastructure. In some cases, courts have dismissed or acquitted defendants where it was shown that actions were peaceful or politically motivated acts of conscience, reflecting a domestic judiciary's cautious approach to infringing political protest.

Digitally, neutrality advocates using social media may face indirect risks under Ireland's cybercrime laws, such as the Criminal Justice (Offences Relating to Information Systems) Act 2017, which criminalizes unauthorized access and disruption of data. While the neutrality movement does not advocate such tactics, increased surveillance or classification of certain digital activism as "disruptive" could criminalize online organizing under broad national security pretexts. Moreover, counter-terrorism cooperation with EU and U.S. partners raises questions about the monitoring of Irish citizens engaging in foreign policy dissent, even when lawfully expressed.

Internationally, the movement benefits from UN declarations affirming the role of civil society in promoting peace. UN General Assembly Resolution A/RES/53/144, which adopted the Declaration on Human Rights Defenders, recognizes individuals and groups who peacefully promote the realization of human rights—including peace and demilitarization—as essential actors entitled to protection from state retaliation.

Thus, while Ireland maintains strong formal protections for peaceful activism, the legal framework is vulnerable to politicization, particularly where national defense or foreign relations are invoked. The legality of protest and expression is shaped not only by statutory language, but by policing discretion, judicial interpretation, and political will. Any effort to suppress or surveil the neutrality movement risks violating both domestic constitutional rights and international civil liberties standards, opening Ireland to legal challenge before domestic courts or international forums, such as the European Court of Human Rights (EctHR). To avoid such outcomes, future policy reform should explicitly safeguard the right to neutrality-based dissent, both offline and online, as a protected form of democratic engagement.

The irish neutrality movement draws much of its momentum from below—driven not by institutional machinery but by civil society's enduring belief in peace as national character. This movement includes artists, educators, youth organizations, veterans, and community leaders who use both tradition and technology to advocate for non-alignment. Street murals in Galway, poetry in Dublin, and student-led teach-ins across the country all contribute to an emergent civic folklore of peace. Digital activism, too, has redefined the battlefield—memes, documentaries, and viral speeches serve as tools for consciousness-raising among younger generations. The emotional tone of the movement—marked by pride, betrayal, and fear of quiet erosion—makes it deeply human. It is a form of cultural resistance, asserting that neutrality is not bureaucratic footnote but public inheritance. These decentralized actions create a distributed guardianship over neutrality, ensuring that no single government, regardless of mandate, can dissolve it without protest from the nation's cultural heart.

7

NATO: VILLIAN OR HERO

Since its foundation in 1949, NATO has stood as a symbol of collective security in the West. Celebrated by some as a protector of democratic values and deterrent against aggression, NATO is condemned by others as a militarized extension of Western geopolitical ambitions. This duality has become especially pronounced since the Cold War, as NATO expanded beyond its initial remit of territorial defense to engage in out-of-area interventions—some with UN Security Council approval, others without.

NATO's defenders argue that the alliance adapts to emerging threats—such as terrorism, state collapse, and mass atrocities—by acting swiftly where the international community fails. Yet, its critics highlight the high civilian toll of its airstrikes, its reliance on legally ambiguous justifications, and a recurring pattern of regime change followed by state failure. These accusations are not merely political; they invoke serious legal and moral questions about the right to intervene and the consequences of doing so.

This chapter explores NATO's evolving role through key case studies, assessing whether the alliance has stayed true to its founding principles or become an unaccountable instrument of force. It evaluates NATO's formation, its transformation, and the ethical and legal controversies that shadow its interventions. Central to this analysis is a consideration of how NATO justifies its actions and whether such justifications withstand legal scrutiny.

NATO was created in the immediate aftermath of the Second World War, amid growing tension between the Western Allies and the Soviet Union. Its primary aim was to deter Soviet expansion and to ensure mutual protection among member states. The North Atlantic Treaty, signed in Washington, D.C., on 4 April 1949, grounded NATO in the principles of the United Nations Charter, emphasizing peaceful dispute resolution and the right of collective self-defense.

The cornerstone of NATO is Article 5, which states that an armed attack on one member is considered an attack on all. While designed to prevent aggression rather than provoke it, the clause created a powerful framework for military solidarity. To date, Article 5 has only been invoked once—in response to the September 11 attacks in 2001. However, NATO's operations in places like Kosovo and Libya were not tied to Article 5. Instead, they relied on broader, more contested doctrines such as humanitarian intervention and the responsibility to protect (R2P).

NATO's formation also carried ideological weight. It was more than a military alliance; it was a political declaration of commitment to liberal democracy, individual rights, and the rule of law. The treaty's preamble reflects this, stating the alliance's intent to safeguard "the freedom, common heritage and civilization of their peoples." These lofty aims would soon be tested in practice.

As the Cold War progressed, NATO functioned primarily as a deterrent force. Its legitimacy, at least during this early phase, was rarely questioned in legal terms. It operated within a clearly defined threat environment, defending the territorial boundaries of its members. But with the collapse of the Soviet Union, the alliance faced an existential question: if its original adversary no longer existed, what was NATO for?

Rather than dissolve or retreat, NATO chose to expand its geographical scope and strategic mandate. This shift marked the beginning of an era where NATO would intervene militarily not only in response to direct attacks but to shape international outcomes abroad. The implications of this transformation—legal, political, and humanitarian—are central to understanding NATO's complex legacy today.

NATO's post-Cold War expansion fundamentally altered the security landscape of Europe. From its original 12 members in 1949, the alliance has grown to include 31 countries—many of which were once part of the Warsaw Pact or the Soviet Union itself. Supporters argue this expansion has promoted democracy, economic reform, and peace in post-Communist states. Yet the consequences have been far more complex, particularly in relation to Russia.

The most sensitive flashpoint stems from perceived Western assurances in the early 1990s that NATO would not move "one inch eastward" beyond a reunified Germany. While these promises were never codified in treaty form, declassified records suggest that such understandings were discussed between Western and Soviet leaders. NATO maintains that no formal commitment was made, but Russia has long cited these discussions as evidence of betrayal—an accusation that has fueled hostility and military aggression, most notably in Georgia (2008) and Ukraine (2014 and 2022).

From 1999 onward, new rounds of accession brought in Poland, Hungary, the Czech Republic, the Baltic states, and others. Each expansion was accompanied by pledges of collective defense under Article 5 and increased military cooperation, including joint exercises near Russian borders. This growing proximity has prompted Russia to treat NATO not merely as a defensive alliance, but as an encroaching threat.

Internally, expansion has raised concerns about NATO's operational unity. With a more diverse membership and divergent national interests, consensus on military action has become harder to achieve. Strategic overreach, underfunded obligations, and political fragmentation among members have complicated NATO's decision-making and effectiveness in rapidly unfolding crises.

From the outside, NATO's expansion has also cast doubt on its strategic motives. Was the alliance responding to requests for protection from vulnerable democracies—or was it projecting power into Russia's sphere of influence? The ambiguity remains, but the impact is clear: NATO's eastward movement has become a defining factor in modern geopolitical instability.

NATO's legitimacy rests on its alignment with international law, most notably the UN Charter, which permits the use of force only in self-defense (Article 51) or with Security Council approval. While NATO frequently invokes these principles, many of its interventions have operated in legal grey zones—exploiting ambiguities in international law or acting without formal authorization.

The 1999 bombing of Yugoslavia, NATO's first major warfighting operation, did not have UN Security Council approval. The alliance justified the campaign as a humanitarian necessity to halt ethnic cleansing in Kosovo. Though NATO claimed moral urgency, the legality of the action remains widely debated. Proponents framed it as an ethical imperative; critics saw it as a breach of sovereignty and a violation of the UN Charter's prohibition on the unilateral use of force.

In contrast, the 2011 intervention in Libya began with explicit Security Council authorization—UNSC Resolution 1973—which permitted the use of force to protect civilians. However, NATO's interpretation of the mandate quickly shifted from protection to regime change. Airstrikes extended beyond military targets to cripple Libya's state infrastructure, culminating in the death of Muammar Gaddafi. This "mission creep" eroded trust in NATO's adherence to legal constraints and called into question the sincerity of humanitarian justifications.

The use of controversial weapons, such as cluster munitions, depleted uranium shells, and white phosphorus, by NATO or its members, further complicates the alliance's legal and ethical standing. While not explicitly banned in all contexts under international law, their use in populated areas may violate principles of proportionality and distinction under international humanitarian law. Investigations into such actions have rarely resulted in prosecutions or accountability.

Additionally, NATO's structural model insulates it from direct legal scrutiny. As an alliance of sovereign states rather than a legal person or entity, NATO itself cannot be tried in court. Responsibility is diffused among its members, many of whom invoke national security to avoid transparency or judicial oversight. This has led to widespread criticism that NATO operates under de facto immunity, shielded from the accountability expected of states or even non-state actors.

Ethically, NATO's interventions raise enduring questions. Can humanitarian aims justify illegal force? Can democratic values be exported by bombing campaigns? And who is responsible when things go wrong—when civilian casualties mount, or when post-conflict chaos follows? These are not merely academic questions. They strike at the core of NATO's credibility and whether it represents a genuine force for international order or a geopolitical actor cloaked in the language of law and morality.

NATO's bombing campaign against the Federal Republic of Yugoslavia in 1999—Operation Allied Force—was a watershed moment for the alliance. It marked NATO's first sustained military action without the explicit authorization of the UN Security Council, setting a precedent for future interventions justified on humanitarian grounds.

The campaign arose from escalating violence in Kosovo, where Serbian forces under Slobodan Milošević were accused of ethnic cleansing against Kosovar Albanians. The immediate trigger was the controversial Račak incident, in which Serbian paramilitaries allegedly executed dozens of ethnic Albanians. While Western observers declared it a massacre, forensic reviews—including a Finnish-led investigation—raised questions about the circumstances, leading some to suspect it was used to justify intervention.

NATO launched airstrikes in March 1999, arguing that diplomacy had failed and that urgent military action was required to prevent further atrocities. Over 78 days, NATO aircraft flew more than 38,000 sorties. Civilian infrastructure—including bridges, factories, television stations, and utilities—was heavily bombed. One of the most controversial attacks was the April 23 bombing of Radio Television Serbia (RTS) in Belgrade, which killed 16 media workers. NATO claimed the station was part of the Yugoslav propaganda apparatus; human rights organizations condemned the strike as a war crime.

Estimates suggest around 500 civilian deaths, though numbers vary. NATO used cluster munitions in urban areas and depleted uranium shells, raising long-term health and environmental concerns. The bombing of a passenger train at Grdelica Gorge and a refugee convoy near Djakovica highlighted the risks of conducting a high-altitude air campaign with limited ground intelligence.

The campaign ended with the withdrawal of Serbian forces from Kosovo and the deployment of a UN peacekeeping mission (UNMIK) and NATO-led KFOR. While some hailed the intervention as a successful humanitarian mission, it remains legally and morally contentious. Without Security Council backing, the operation arguably violated Article 2(4) of the UN Charter, which prohibits the use of force against a sovereign state unless in self-defense or with Council approval.

NATO's defense rested on moral legitimacy rather than legal authority, advancing the controversial doctrine of humanitarian intervention. However, the legal vacuum and selective nature of such interventions have led many to question NATO's consistency and motives, especially given its inaction in contemporaneous crises elsewhere.

NATO's involvement in Afghanistan began in the wake of the September 11, 2001 terrorist attacks, when the alliance invoked Article 5 for the first and only time. This paved the way for NATO's formal role in the U.S.-led campaign against the Taliban and Al-Qaeda, culminating in the deployment of the International Security Assistance Force (ISAF) in 2003.

What began as a mission to stabilize Kabul evolved into a sprawling military occupation with over 50 NATO and partner nations engaged across the country. ISAF's mandate expanded to include counter-insurgency, state-building, and support for the Afghan government—ambitions that far exceeded the alliance's prior military scope.

NATO's two-decade involvement was marred by civilian casualties, reliance on warlord proxies, and fluctuating strategic objectives. One of the most damning episodes was the 2009 Kunduz airstrike, ordered by a German officer, which killed dozens of civilians after NATO forces bombed fuel tankers stolen by insurgents. Though intended as a tactical strike, it caused a major political backlash in Germany and exposed NATO's vulnerability to flawed intelligence and escalation.

The alliance's cooperation with various Afghan strongmen, many with histories of human rights abuses, drew criticism from international monitors. These alliances were justified as necessary for regional control but undermined the broader mission of promoting democratic governance and rule of law.

Despite vast expenditures in both blood and treasure, NATO's presence failed to prevent the Taliban's resurgence. Following the U.S. and NATO withdrawal in 2021, the Afghan government collapsed rapidly, with Taliban forces retaking control in a matter of weeks. The images of evacuation chaos in Kabul, including NATO forces abandoning local allies, became a symbol of strategic failure and diplomatic disengagement.

Supporters of the intervention argue that NATO helped deny terrorist groups a safe haven for two decades and supported vital infrastructure, education, and women's rights programs. But the long-term sustainability of these gains is now in doubt. The war in Afghanistan has become a case study in the limits of military power in state-building and the fragility of externally imposed institutions.

From a legal perspective, NATO's role in Afghanistan was anchored in Security Council resolutions and Article 5 legitimacy. But the operational execution—marked by blurred lines between military and civilian targets, controversial drone strikes, and detainee abuses—invites questions about compliance with international humanitarian law.

The Afghanistan campaign remains the alliance's longest and most complex engagement. It exposed internal divisions among NATO members, strategic drift, and operational overstretch—casting doubt on the alliance's ability to deliver sustainable outcomes in future global interventions.

NATO's 2011 military intervention in Libya, under the banner of Operation Unified Protector, began with broad international support. The campaign was launched in response to a civil uprising against Muammar Gaddafi, whose forces were accused of targeting civilians in rebel-held areas such as Benghazi. The United Nations Security Council passed Resolution 1973, authorizing member states to enforce a no-fly zone and take "all necessary measures" to protect civilians. This legal cover marked a rare instance of formal UN authorization for NATO military action.

What followed, however, quickly departed from the spirit—if not the letter—of that resolution. NATO interpreted the mandate expansively, shifting its focus from civilian protection to active support for the rebels, including the targeting of government compounds, supply routes, and eventually Gaddafi himself. This widening of objectives—commonly referred to as "mission creep"—sparked accusations that NATO had overstepped its legal bounds, transforming a defensive operation into a campaign for regime change.

Gaddafi was ultimately captured and killed by rebel forces in Sirte in October 2011, ending the decades-long rule of one of Africa's most notorious strongmen. But the vacuum that followed plunged Libya into political chaos, with rival militias, tribal factions, and jihadist groups vying for control. The absence of a post-conflict stabilization plan mirrored earlier

Western missteps in Iraq and Afghanistan and led to a prolonged humanitarian and security crisis.

Human rights observers documented reprisal killings, arbitrary detentions, and torture committed by NATO-backed rebel factions. These abuses went largely unacknowledged by NATO, which disclaimed responsibility for the conduct of local ground forces. Critics argue this selective accountability undermines the alliance's credibility and violates its stated principles of protecting human rights and civilian life.

In retrospect, the Libya intervention is often cited as a textbook case of how quickly humanitarian justifications can evolve into political agendas. While NATO maintained it acted to avert a massacre in Benghazi, the operational outcome was the violent overthrow of a government—raising legal and ethical questions about the legitimacy of its actions.

Libya remains a fractured state, its institutions weakened, its economy crippled, and its society divided. For many, this outcome casts a long shadow over the notion that NATO can responsibly lead humanitarian interventions without a coherent and binding post-conflict framework.

Beyond its public operations, NATO's post-9/11 engagement in the "War on Terror" intersected with covert activities involving extraordinary rendition, secret detention sites, and torture—largely conducted by the United States but facilitated by several NATO allies. These programs were never officially authorized by NATO as an organization, yet they occurred with the knowledge and cooperation of key member states.

Investigations by the Council of Europe, Amnesty International, and investigative journalists uncovered a network of CIA "black sites"—covert prisons located in countries such as Poland, Lithuania, and Romania, where detainees were subjected to interrogation techniques widely considered to be torture. Practices included waterboarding, sensory deprivation, stress positions, and sleep disruption. In many cases, detainees were held without charge or legal representation.

While NATO itself denies any direct operational role, its members' complicity in hosting, facilitating, or ignoring these activities has raised serious questions about the alliance's moral integrity. The European Court of Human Rights has issued rulings condemning member states for violations of international human rights law, including arbitrary detention and the denial of due process.

The broader issue is one of institutional silence and collective denial. No NATO state has held senior officials accountable for their role in these practices. Internal reviews, where conducted, were narrow in scope and typically shielded by claims of national security. Legal redress has been slow and symbolic, with most victims of rendition still denied access to justice or reparations.

These black site operations not only violated the Convention Against Torture, to which NATO members are signatories, but also undermined the foundational values of the alliance—namely, the rule of law and protection of individual liberties. The use of torture-tainted intelligence also raises operational concerns: such information is unreliable, legally inadmissible, and strategically damaging when exposed.

The ethical cost of these clandestine activities has been high. They have eroded NATO's moral standing, weakened its legitimacy as a global security actor, and provided propaganda ammunition to authoritarian regimes and extremist groups alike. More fundamentally, they challenge the idea that NATO can both fight terrorism and uphold human rights without contradiction.

To date, there has been no comprehensive reckoning within NATO on the extent of complicity in post-9/11 abuses. Without meaningful transparency and accountability, the alliance risks repeating the same mistakes under new guises—where legality becomes subordinate to expedience, and moral leadership is lost in the shadows.

Following the 1999 bombing campaign against Yugoslavia, NATO's responsibilities in Kosovo transitioned from warfighting to peacekeeping through the Kosovo Force (KFOR). Tasked with stabilizing the region and ensuring civilian safety, KFOR's mandate was to uphold UN Security Council Resolution 1244. Yet the post-war environment quickly revealed the challenges of navigating ethnic hostility, political fragmentation, and impunity for wartime conduct.

Although Serbian forces withdrew from the province, violence did not end. In the power vacuum that followed, ethnic Albanians conducted retaliatory attacks against Serbs and Roma minorities. Thousands were displaced. Despite the presence of international peacekeepers, over 200,000 Serbs and Roma fled Kosovo, many never to return. NATO's inability—or unwillingness—to prevent this reverse-ethnic cleansing has drawn widespread condemnation and cast a shadow over the legitimacy of its presence.

Equally disturbing were the allegations of organ trafficking raised in a 2010 report by the Council of Europe. The report implicated members of the Kosovo Liberation Army (KLA)—key NATO allies during the conflict—in the abduction and killing of Serbian prisoners for the illicit sale of organs. While evidence remains contested, the seriousness of the allegations demands attention. Yet to date, no high-level prosecutions have resulted from these claims.

KFOR, though operationally successful in deterring further state-level conflict, failed to build long-term reconciliation or enforce consistent rule of law. Kosovo declared independence in 2008, a move recognized by many NATO members but not by Serbia, Russia, or a number of UN states—ensuring the region remains diplomatically and politically unsettled.

The Kosovo experience reflects a recurring pattern: NATO interventions frequently achieve short-term military or political goals but struggle with post-conflict governance, justice, and long-term stability. NATO's dependence on local factions—some with histories of abuse—further undermines its credibility as a neutral actor committed to civilian protection and democratic norms.

In both official and proxy campaigns, NATO and its member states have deployed weaponry that has generated intense legal and humanitarian debate. Chief among them are cluster munitions, depleted uranium (DU) shells, and white phosphorus—weapons whose use in populated areas risks violating the fundamental principles of international humanitarian law (IHL).

During the 1999 Kosovo campaign, NATO admitted to dropping over 1,300 cluster bombs, including in urban areas like Niš and Belgrade. Cluster munitions disperse hundreds of small bomblets over a wide area, many of which fail to explode on impact and function like landmines. Civilians, particularly children, often fall victim to these unexploded remnants years after the conflict ends. Despite increasing global pressure, NATO has not committed to the Convention on Cluster Munitions, citing operational necessity and adherence to its own internal guidelines.

NATO's use of depleted uranium shells has also attracted criticism. While DU enhances armor-piercing capacity, it is chemically toxic and slightly radioactive. Studies in Kosovo, Iraq, and the Balkans have raised concerns about long-term health effects, including cancer clusters in areas with heavy DU deployment. Though NATO maintains DU is safe when used correctly, the absence of long-term monitoring and remediation efforts undermines public trust.

White phosphorus—a chemical that ignites on contact with oxygen—has been used by NATO member states, notably the United States, in conflicts like Iraq and Afghanistan. While technically permitted under IHL when used for illumination or smoke cover, its use in civilian areas has caused severe burns, disfigurement, and death. In Fallujah and elsewhere, the use of white phosphorus raised accusations of indiscriminate attacks in violation of the Geneva Conventions.

The legal ambiguity surrounding these weapons often hinges on intended use and targeting protocols, but the moral cost is harder to obscure. NATO has rarely investigated or acknowledged the long-term consequences of these deployments. Civilian populations have borne the brunt of contamination, injury, and death—often without compensation, apology, or accountability.

The enduring presence of unexploded munitions and environmental damage caused by NATO campaigns contradicts the alliance's stated commitment to civilian protection. The repeated use of controversial weaponry not only raises ethical red flags but also opens the door to potential legal liability under evolving customary and treaty-based international law.

Throughout its evolution, NATO has operated in a shifting legal terrain defined by UN Charter principles, evolving doctrines like Responsibility to Protect (R2P), and state practice. While some operations—such as Afghanistan (post-2001) and Libya (2011, initially)—were launched with UN Security Council resolutions, others, notably the Yugoslavia 1999 campaign, proceeded without formal UN authorization. This selective approach to legal mandates has eroded the perception of NATO as a rules-based actor.

Key legal tensions include:

UN Charter Article 2(4) prohibits the use of force against sovereign states without Security Council approval or in self-defense. NATO's Kosovo campaign violated this prohibition in letter, if not in perceived moral justification.

UN Charter Article 51, which permits self-defense, was used legitimately after 9/11 to justify NATO's engagement in Afghanistan. Yet, the prolonged occupation and civilian toll challenged NATO's ability to remain within lawful military parameters.

The evolving doctrine of "humanitarian intervention"—arguably used in Kosovo and stretched in Libya—remains controversial in international law, lacking universal recognition as a legal norm.

NATO's use of controversial weapons may contravene Additional Protocols I and II of the Geneva Conventions, which prohibit indiscriminate attacks and demand proportionality in targeting. The burden of proof, however, lies with victims who often lack access to legal remedy.

The alliance's institutional structure limits legal accountability. NATO, as a collective entity, is not a party to international treaties, making enforcement difficult. Member states shift responsibility, and international courts have so far declined to prosecute NATO actions or omissions.

The result is a system where NATO frequently operates in zones of legal ambiguity, protected by power dynamics, political consensus among members, and the absence of enforceable oversight. This immunity has invited calls for reform—from clearer international mandates to the establishment of independent mechanisms for investigating civilian harm and operational legality.

NATO's journey from a Cold War defense pact to a 21st-century interventionist alliance has been marked by significant strategic, ethical, and legal transformation. While the alliance was born from the rubble of World War II as a deterrent to Soviet aggression, its post-1990s operations have increasingly tested the limits of international law and global tolerance for military unilateralism cloaked in collective legitimacy.

The interventions in Yugoslavia, Afghanistan, and Libya illustrate both NATO's ability to project power and its vulnerability to mission creep, collateral damage, and post-conflict disorder. In Kosovo, NATO acted without UN authorization. In Libya, it exceeded its mandate. In Afghanistan, its engagement stretched across two decades with unclear end goals and mixed results. NATO's tactical strengths—air supremacy, technological coordination, and unified command—have not always translated into durable peace or lawful conduct.

Moreover, the use of controversial weaponry, the hosting of black sites, and the failure to hold perpetrators accountable have weakened NATO's credibility as a moral force in global security. The alliance's lack of direct legal accountability, coupled with ambiguous interpretation of international mandates, creates a perception of selective justice—one that undermines the rules-based order NATO purports to defend.

As NATO expands its scope, shatters borders, and redefines the meaning of collective defense, one question should confront every neutral nation—especially Ireland: *Can we trust NATO?*

For decades, Ireland has maintained a proud tradition of neutrality—not as a passive stance, but as a principled position rooted in diplomacy, peacekeeping, and moral independence. NATO, by contrast, operates with increasing disregard for legal boundaries or unified international consent. It bypasses the UN Security Council, justifies military campaigns on shifting moral grounds, and leaves devastated regions in its wake.

NATO has become—at times—not a disciplined alliance, but a cartel of war-ready governments, willing to use force without due oversight, often enabled by arms manufacturers eager to arm any regime or faction with the right budget. In this climate, law is bent, accountability is evaded, and the line between liberator and occupier is blurred. Some of NATO's operations resemble the Wild West more than a rules-based international system.

Ireland, if it were to join NATO, would not only become party to this dynamic—it would become a target. Once a member, Ireland would lose the diplomatic insulation that neutrality provides. It would be expected to contribute militarily, endorse controversial missions, and become a conduit for arms and surveillance infrastructure. In doing so, it risks becoming entangled in "forever wars" driven not by justice but by the geopolitics of dominant member states and the profit margins of defense contractors.

The core question is no longer abstract. It is urgent, tangible, and existential:

Can Ireland trust NATO with its reputation, its values, its neutrality, and its future?

To abandon neutrality for alignment with an increasingly unregulated war-fighting coalition would be to gamble Ireland's global image, its moral clarity, and its ability to act as an independent voice on the world stage.

If NATO cannot regulate its actions, prosecute its crimes, or restrain its impulses, then Ireland has every reason—and every right—to remain outside its grasp.

Ireland's prestige does not lie in firepower or alliances. It lies in diplomacy, credibility, and the ability to speak to all sides without being an accessory to destruction. In a world torn between militarism and sovereignty, Ireland's neutrality is not a weakness—it is its strength. And it must be defended.

The final question remains:
If Ireland lies down with NATO—will it rise with its values, or with its shame?

8

IRELAND, NATO AND THE EU

Ireland is not a NATO member, but it does not exist outside NATO's influence. Since joining the Partnership for Peace (PfP) in 1999, Ireland has quietly but steadily deepened its cooperation with the alliance. Though presented as a voluntary program focused on peacekeeping, humanitarian training, and disaster response, PfP increasingly acts as a gateway to alignment with NATO's military and political priorities.

The Irish government maintains that PfP does not compromise neutrality. Yet, repeated participation in NATO-led exercises, shared operational frameworks, and joint military training have blurred those assurances. These activities are frequently justified under the umbrella of peacekeeping or crisis management, but they often mirror NATO's own strategic goals, subtly redefining Ireland's defense posture without formal treaty obligations.

As noted in **Chapter 7** on NATO, this quiet integration has real-world implications. Involvement in exercises or missions with NATO members risks entanglement in conflicts where Ireland has no national interest. The concern is not hypothetical. It reflects a growing unease among scholars and neutral policy advocates who see PfP as a tool of incremental militarisation, facilitating NATO's influence through cooperation rather than formal membership.

Moreover, NATO's dominance over Europe's security architecture often means that non-members must align their own policies with the alliance's agenda to maintain relevance or funding within broader regional frameworks. This pressure, while informal, is nonetheless effective—and it raises a fundamental question for Ireland: How much of neutrality remains if one's military doctrine is shaped by an alliance one has not joined?

If NATO casts a long shadow, the European Union's push for military integration brings the challenge to Ireland's neutrality into even sharper relief. Since the launch of PESCO (Permanent Structured Cooperation) in 2017, EU defense has shifted from aspiration to mechanism. Ireland is now participating in a formalized military cooperation structure that includes shared defense spending targets, joint weapons development, and collaborative military operations.

PESCO is not technically a standing EU army, but it introduces binding commitments and blurs the distinction between civilian EU governance and military cooperation. These commitments are not just financial—they are strategic. Member states must pledge to increase defense capabilities, standardize procedures, and harmonize with broader EU goals, many of which are developed in coordination with NATO.

The Irish government insists that participation in select PESCO projects respects Ireland's policy of neutrality. But the lack of transparency in how these decisions are made—combined with the overlap between PESCO goals and NATO strategies—undermines public trust. Critics argue that mission creep is inevitable: that today's collaborative research project could become tomorrow's logistical contribution to a joint military intervention.

The companion initiative, the European Defence Fund (EDF), finances the development of new weapons systems and military technologies—another subtle departure from neutrality. Although Ireland is not obligated to manufacture weapons, its participation supports a system that promotes military-industrial integration, placing profit and strategic interoperability ahead of diplomatic restraint. Supporters of deeper integration argue that Europe faces serious threats—hybrid warfare, terrorism, and renewed Russian aggression—and that Ireland must play its part in collective defense. But the reality is that Ireland is not a frontline state, nor does it face imminent military danger requiring large-scale alignment. Its most valuable contributions to global stability have historically come through UN peacekeeping, conflict mediation, and moral diplomacy, not through force projection.

Neutrality has given Ireland a distinctive and respected voice on the international stage. The more deeply Ireland embeds itself in military alliances—even under the guise of cooperation—the more it sacrifices that independence. The symbolic weight of neutrality is more than diplomatic; it informs how Ireland is perceived and how it acts. It is a safeguard against entanglement and a statement of principle in a world increasingly ruled by blocs and hard power. Abandoning neutrality could also carry economic and security costs. If Ireland joins military ventures led by the EU or NATO, it may become a strategic target. In the current global environment, where cyberattacks, critical infrastructure sabotage, and economic retaliation are tools of statecraft, neutrality offers a form of protection. As a NATO member, Ireland's position would shift from observer to stakeholder—along with all the risks that entails.

Furthermore, neutrality allows Ireland to maintain an arms-length relationship with the global arms industry, which is often driven more by market demand than moral discretion. As history shows, NATO-aligned militaries frequently supply regimes with questionable human rights records, fueling conflict rather than containing it. If Ireland were to become a full military partner, it would be expected to fall in line with these decisions—or risk isolation within the alliance.

Ireland's neutrality has long stood as both a strategic doctrine and a moral compass—an active expression of independence, not a passive abstention from war. But that position is now facing its greatest test. Through NATO-aligned cooperation and increasing entanglement in European Union military structures, the legal, political, and operational boundaries that have historically protected Irish neutrality are being eroded, not by overt declarations of war, but through procedural creep and political ambiguity.

Under Bunreacht na hÉireann—the Irish Constitution—sovereignty is a foundational principle. While neutrality is not expressly codified, Articles 1 through 5 and Article 29.4 make clear that the delegation of sovereign powers to foreign institutions must be subject to a referendum if it alters the State's autonomy. Yet deeper alignment with NATO through the Partnership for Peace and integration into EU defense mechanisms via PESCO (Permanent Structured Cooperation) and the European Defence Fund (EDF) may, under a strict constitutional interpretation, cross that threshold. What is unfolding may not be illegal by statute, but it arguably violates the intent and spirit of constitutional safeguards meant to prevent precisely this kind of strategic realignment without public consent.

The Triple Lock mechanism—established in 2001 as a procedural guarantee of Ireland's neutrality—requires that any overseas deployment of Irish troops receive approval from the government, the Dáil Éireann, and, crucially, a United Nations Security Council resolution. This tri-layered approval process ensures that military action is not taken unilaterally or in alignment with any bloc whose agenda might differ from Ireland's national interest. Yet, in recent years, there has been mounting political pressure to dismantle this protection. Those advocating for deeper EU-NATO military cooperation have cast the Triple Lock as an obstacle rather than a safeguard, threatening to remove one of the few remaining constitutional bulwarks against automatic engagement in foreign conflicts.

On the international plane, Ireland is a signatory to the United Nations Charter. Under Article 2(4), the use of force is strictly prohibited unless exercised in self-defense or authorized by the Security Council. Article 51 reaffirms the right of self-defense but within narrow legal limits. NATO's historical pattern of intervention without explicit UN mandates, such as in Yugoslavia in 1999 and Libya in 2011, puts Ireland at risk of association with operations that violate these principles. If Ireland were drawn into such actions through joint defense structures or logistical support, it could be in breach of international law—not as a combatant, but as a cooperator.

The Lisbon Treaty of 2009 further complicates matters. While Ireland secured a formal opt-out from the EU's mutual defense clause under Article 42.7 of the Treaty on European Union, its participation in PESCO and EDF may undercut that opt-out in practice. These frameworks re-integrate Ireland into European defense planning through parallel mechanisms that bypass the political scrutiny which a full treaty obligation would trigger. This amounts to legal circumvention, leaving the public without a clear understanding of the commitments being made on its behalf, or their long-term consequences.

Even if Irish troops are not deployed directly into combat, there are other forms of complicity to consider. Under the Geneva Conventions and the rules of international humanitarian law, logistical or material support to missions involving unlawful acts—such as indiscriminate bombing, disproportionate force, or collaboration with actors engaged in war crimes—could expose Ireland to reputational and legal consequences. The principle of command responsibility is increasingly applied to indirect participants, not just those giving orders or pulling triggers.

On the administrative level, Ireland is subject to elements of the EU Defence Procurement Directive (2009/81/EC), which encourages harmonization of defense contracts among member states. As Ireland becomes more involved in EU-led projects, the political and financial pressure to purchase compatible weapons systems or infrastructure could intensify, gradually shifting procurement policy away from national discretion and into the realm of industrial interdependence. This further ties Ireland's defense posture to decisions made outside its borders—without democratic accountability, and often in service of a wider geopolitical agenda.

What emerges from all of this is not merely a legal argument but a constitutional and strategic crossroads. Ireland is not simply being invited into military cooperation—it is being absorbed into it, procedurally and politically, without the national debate or legal clarity that such a transformation requires. The notion that neutrality is still intact becomes harder to sustain when the legal mechanisms designed to protect it are either being dismantled or reinterpreted to allow for exceptions that increasingly resemble alignment.

The danger is not that Ireland will declare war, but that it will wake up one day to find that it has given away the legal tools it once used to resist one.

Neutrality is often dismissed as outdated in today's fractured world—a quaint ideal in the age of hybrid warfare and supranational defense policy. But that dismissal misunderstands what neutrality actually provides. It is not isolationist; it is a strategy of independence. It gives Ireland room to mediate rather than mobilize, to lead diplomatically rather than follow militarily, and to operate under its own compass rather than under the strategic whims of others. It is not the absence of commitment—it is the refusal to have that commitment dictated by others.

What remains now is not just the legal architecture of neutrality, but the political courage to defend it. If Ireland lets go of that courage, if it allows neutrality to be undermined by partnership agreements, back-door alignments, or legislative vagueness, then it will have lost more than policy. It will have lost a piece of its constitutional sovereignty, its moral credibility, and its strategic independence.

And once neutrality is lost, it may not be law—or even war—that brings it back. It will take a reckoning.

Ireland must decide: does it retain the authority to set its own course in matters of war and peace, or does it surrender that authority to alliances with agendas not its own? Neutrality is not merely worth defending—it is the very definition of Ireland's right to decide.

9

IRELAND'S STRATEGIC POSITION AS A NATO MEMBER

Ireland's geographic position on the western edge of Europe gives it outsized strategic value within the North Atlantic security landscape. Although Ireland is not currently a NATO member, its proximity to transatlantic undersea cables, its Atlantic ports, and its position as the closest European landmass to North America already make it a point of military interest. As a full NATO member, Ireland would likely become more than a supporting voice—it would become a logistical and intelligence hub.

Ireland's airspace and ports would be repurposed not just for civilian and commercial access, but for high-priority military transit. Shannon Airport, already a known refueling stop for U.S. military flights, would become an openly integrated logistics platform for NATO deployment operations. Ports like Cork, Foynes, and Dublin could be adapted for naval staging or maintenance facilities. Intelligence-sharing would likely deepen under

NATO's common security frameworks, making Ireland a key listening post between European and U.S. defense operations.

Ireland's role in cyber and digital defense would also expand dramatically. With a disproportionate share of Europe's internet traffic routed through its data centers and transatlantic cables, and with global tech giants headquartered in Dublin, Ireland would be positioned as a strategic node in NATO's cyber command grid. Rather than a passive conduit, Ireland could become central to threat detection, surveillance coordination, and information warfare countermeasures.

However, such strategic elevation comes at a cost. The more essential Ireland becomes to NATO operations, the more likely it is to be perceived as a legitimate military target in the event of a wider conflict. Its undersea cables, refueling hubs, and ports—critical to the alliance's infrastructure—would become targets for sabotage, cyber intrusion, or missile strikes. This is not theoretical positioning; it is the practical outcome of NATO's mutual defense calculus.

With full NATO membership, Ireland would no longer sit out geopolitical confrontations as an observer. It would be a full participant in an alliance designed for collective defense and deterrence—an alliance whose presence in Eastern Europe has repeatedly drawn sharp reactions from adversaries like Russia. That repositioning would mean Ireland's neutral status no longer offers any protection from retaliation in times of conflict.

The strategic exposure is not limited to conventional warfare. Cyber operations, now central to both NATO and Russian military doctrine, would likely target Ireland's tech infrastructure in the event of escalating tensions. Attacks could aim at disrupting NATO's communications or disabling Irish data centers that serve both civilian and military purposes. Such intrusions, beyond being acts of aggression, could also cripple Ireland's economy given its heavy reliance on foreign direct investment and digital exports.

Additionally, NATO membership could invite asymmetric responses from adversaries. These include disinformation campaigns aimed at destabilizing Irish public opinion, economic retaliation, sanctions, or covert political interference. For a small nation deeply embedded in global trade, the cascading effects of becoming a military target could erode not only security but political and economic sovereignty.

Ireland's infrastructure would also likely be drawn into NATO's integrated defense planning. Submarine activity off Ireland's western coast may increase—both friendly and adversarial—due to the concentration of undersea cables, surveillance interest, and Atlantic monitoring operations. Any NATO installation on Irish soil, including radar facilities or early warning systems, would immediately become a first-strike concern for opponents in the event of a conflict.

Despite the risks, NATO membership carries a suite of material and diplomatic benefits. Chief among these is protection under Article 5 of the NATO treaty—the alliance's mutual defense clause. This guarantee of collective defense transforms every member's vulnerability into a shared obligation. For Ireland, with a limited defense budget and small standing military, the assurance of coordinated NATO response in the face of aggression is a powerful incentive.

In addition, NATO membership would provide access to cutting-edge military technologies, coordinated training exercises, and strategic intelligence. Ireland's Defense Forces, traditionally structured around peacekeeping and domestic roles, would benefit from modernization, strategic alignment, and cross-training with more experienced forces. While

NATO does not require a standing army at scale, it does enable smaller nations to specialize in logistics, cyber, medical, and intelligence support roles.

NATO membership would also strengthen political ties with other Western democracies, consolidating Ireland's position within the broader transatlantic alliance. Economic opportunities might follow: increased defense-sector collaboration, technology contracts, and infrastructural investment could arrive through NATO-funded initiatives. Diplomatically, Ireland could find itself with greater influence in shaping European defense debates—not from the outside as a neutral, but from within as a stakeholder.

But this elevation in status would require sacrificing neutrality. Ireland's foreign policy identity—carefully preserved since independence—would shift from one of autonomous diplomacy to collective alignment. Ireland would no longer be the neutral broker in global peace efforts; it would be a participant in the deterrence strategies of the West.

This policy shift would also introduce domestic political friction. Public support for neutrality remains strong, and NATO membership would likely face legal and constitutional challenges. While there is no explicit neutrality clause in the Irish Constitution, Ireland's foreign policy has historically been guided by Article 29, which emphasizes peaceful resolution of conflicts and cooperation with international institutions. A major realignment with a military bloc may arguably require a public referendum to maintain constitutional integrity.

Should Ireland become a NATO member, its wartime role would likely reflect its existing capabilities: logistical access, cyber support, and humanitarian assistance. Ireland would not field front-line combat divisions, but its strategic facilities—Shannon Airport, deepwater ports, and digital networks—would serve as essential back-end infrastructure for NATO operations in a European theater.

This support role should not be underestimated. In modern warfare, the value of logistics, data, and mobility is equal to that of firepower. NATO would gain from Ireland's geographic location, and Ireland would contribute by enabling the flow of personnel, materiel, and information. It could also provide specialist personnel in engineering, search and rescue, civilian evacuation, and disaster response—areas where Ireland already holds global credentials through UN operations.

Still, reliance on Article 5 as an ultimate deterrent is not without caveats. While the clause obligates NATO members to treat an attack on one as an attack on all, the form of response is discretionary. Each country retains the right to determine how it will fulfill that obligation. There is no automatic commitment to military retaliation. History shows that NATO responses vary depending on the political climate, scale of attack, and strategic interests of dominant members. In other words, Ireland's security would be tied to the political will of larger allies whose priorities may shift over time.

Remaining outside NATO carries its own risks, particularly in a security environment shaped by Russian hostility and transatlantic dependence. But staying outside the alliance also allows Ireland to continue shaping its defense policy in accordance with national interest, not alliance obligation. Neutrality may not offer a formal defense guarantee—but it offers flexibility, legal independence, and a global perception of impartiality.

If Ireland joined NATO, it would not merely cross a diplomatic threshold—it would redefine its constitutional identity and strategic purpose. The shift from neutrality to alliance membership cannot be viewed as a simple security upgrade; it is a fundamental reorientation of the Irish State's role in global affairs. That shift carries immense legal, political, and moral consequences.

Under Bunreacht na hÉireann, Ireland's Constitution does not enshrine neutrality, but it imposes structural safeguards that complicate deep foreign alignment without public consent. Article 29.4 limits the delegation of sovereignty to foreign bodies unless approved through a referendum. Full NATO membership, which includes binding military obligations and operational commitments, could arguably trigger this threshold. Moreover, as a member, Ireland would be bound not only by NATO's founding treaty but by the security interests of its most dominant players—primarily the United States.

Legally, Ireland would also have to reconcile its obligations under the UN Charter, particularly Article 2(4), which prohibits the threat or use of force against other states outside Security Council authorization. NATO has, in multiple instances, acted without such authorization. If Ireland were implicated in these operations, it could breach its international legal commitments.

Militarily, Ireland would be exposed to the risk of attack not as a neutral bystander, but as a participant in a military alliance. Its tech sector, ports, cables, and airports would all become legitimate targets in a modern conflict. Economically, the costs of militarization, strategic vulnerability, and potential retaliatory sanctions would weigh heavily on a country whose prosperity depends on its perception as a stable, neutral hub for investment and diplomacy.

Strategically, NATO membership would trade autonomy for alliance, and moral clarity for strategic ambiguity. Ireland would no longer control the conditions under which it goes to war—it would react to collective decisions shaped by powers with far greater military reach and political influence.

10

UNDERSEA CABLES
DEFENDING DATA OR DEFENDING INTERESTS?

In recent years, the Irish government has increasingly referenced the need to protect critical infrastructure, most notably the undersea internet cables, as justification for reconsidering its long-held stance of neutrality. This framing positions Ireland as vulnerable, a soft underbelly of Western communications infrastructure, open to attack by hostile foreign actors unless it aligns itself militarily, potentially through NATO. At first glance, this may appear reasonable. After all, these fiber-optic cables are vital to global communications, underpinning the internet, financial transactions, and state security. But a deeper examination reveals this narrative to be politically convenient, strategically timed, and potentially misleading. In truth, invoking cable defense may be less about real risk and more about paving the way for a permanent policy shift in Ireland's international posture.

The argument has a certain modern flair: data is the new oil, and its pipelines—these vast underwater cables—are worthy of defense. Yet the alarmism around their safety coincides almost too neatly with growing domestic and international pressure for Ireland to abandon neutrality or, at the very least, dilute it to the point of irrelevance. Rather than lead with an honest debate about national identity, sovereignty, and foreign policy, the government has cloaked this policy pivot in the garb of technological vulnerability. It is no longer about ideals or geopolitics, we are told; it is about safeguarding the servers and routers that keep the nation running.

But it is precisely this sleight of hand that should raise concern. For generations, Irish neutrality has been a cornerstone of the nation's diplomacy, humanitarian identity, and moral independence. If this is to change, it should not be through sleight, spin, or a manufactured crisis. The public deserves clarity, not camouflage. The undersea cable narrative is rapidly becoming a Trojan horse—an excuse that cloaks a more complex and less popular reality. As this chapter will explore, the cables themselves are indeed significant, but their existence does not require Ireland to become entangled in military alliances. The technology is not the threat. The narrative is.

The Irish government and affiliated media have now made frequent reference to undersea cables as if they were geopolitical ticking time bombs. Ireland, by virtue of its location, is home to several key transatlantic cables, including the AEConnect, Hibernia Express, and GTT Atlantic lines. These cables are integral to global data transmission between North America and Europe and serve as digital highways for everything from online banking and encrypted diplomatic communications to Netflix streaming and cloud services. According to government rhetoric, this strategic role now makes

Ireland uniquely exposed to foreign sabotage, with Russia being the most frequently cited shadowy actor.

This framing feels alarmingly convenient. For decades, Ireland has remained outside military alliances, taking pride in a tradition of neutrality that allowed it to operate with a distinct moral identity in global affairs. It supported peacekeeping missions, championed diplomacy, and avoided being entangled in the wars and ambitions of others. Now, under the cover of digital infrastructure anxiety, this position is being reconsidered—not through open debate, but through insinuation. The narrative around cable defense bypasses direct democratic discourse and instead packages neutrality as outdated, even irresponsible.

Yet neutrality has not failed Ireland. On the contrary, it has made it an attractive host for data centers and multinational technology companies. Tech giants like Google, Amazon, Meta, and Microsoft have built and operated large-scale infrastructure in Ireland, not just because of favorable tax policies but also because of Ireland's stable political climate and perceived independence. It is no coincidence that these cables come ashore in a neutral country—neutrality has commercial as well as moral value.

The cables themselves, while critical, are not uniquely at risk. There is no conclusive evidence of active plots to sever Ireland's internet links. Disruptions that do occur are mostly accidental: undersea earthquakes, shipping anchors, and fishing trawlers are far more common culprits than foreign navies or covert divers. These risks are known and largely mitigated by existing systems of redundancy. Data traffic is automatically rerouted, and there are entire consortia of repair vessels, many based in international waters, ready to respond to damage within hours or days.

And it must be emphasized: the vast majority of undersea cables are privately owned. Governments, including Ireland's, do not have primary operational control. Responsibility lies with telecom consortia, infrastructure providers, and technology firms, who already invest in cyber and physical protections. There is no evidence that NATO membership would change this, nor that foreign militaries would or could effectively defend thousands of kilometers of cable running through international waters.

So, what does military alignment offer that civilian infrastructure planning does not? The answer is more political than practical. Joining NATO would not place warships along the cable routes or shield Ireland's digital lifelines from plausible threats. But it would signal compliance with the evolving posture of Western alliances. It would mark the end of Ireland's moral independence and the beginning of its strategic absorption into a larger, more aggressive geopolitical framework. And for what? A danger that, so far, remains more speculative than real.

The narrative of cable defense, then, is less about cables and more about control—control over the national conversation, control over the framing of Ireland's global role, control over the future of Irish neutrality. This is the real threat—not a submarine lurking off the Kerry coast, but a narrative quietly cutting through public resistance, fiber by fiber.

While the undersea cables are certainly important, they are not the only infrastructure vulnerable to modern risks. Yet, they have become uniquely weaponized in Ireland's political discourse. Why? Because they are invisible. They lie at the bottom of the ocean, carry no noise, and are not part of the average citizen's awareness. Their technical complexity makes them perfect for fear-based narratives that cannot be easily challenged or verified. In other words, they are the perfect vessel through which to smuggle geopolitical agendas.

Most citizens would struggle to describe where these cables run, who owns them, or how they work. Fewer still would know what damage might actually look like, or how quickly a repair could occur. In that knowledge vacuum, political operatives and advisors have discovered fertile ground. By emphasizing the hypothetical threat of sabotage, without providing a credible assessment of likelihood or consequence, state actors can build a compelling argument for policy change. It is fear, not fact, that is leading the charge.

To add urgency, officials and media commentators have leaned on the spectre of hybrid warfare—espionage, cyberattacks, and gray-zone tactics where attribution is murky and deterrence is elusive. These concerns are valid in the abstract, but they do not specifically justify military entanglement. Hybrid threats require hybrid responses: regulation, resilience, and civilian intelligence capabilities, not battalions or treaties. Neutral countries like Finland, Switzerland and Austria have long understood this. Their response has been to strengthen infrastructure, not abandon sovereignty.

In fact, before it joined NATO, Finland had among the most robust non-military security systems in Europe. It trained its citizens in civil defense, invested in encrypted digital networks, and developed advanced early-warning systems. Ireland has done none of these things. Instead, it has reached for the most dramatic solution available: foreign military alignment. This leap over more obvious civilian protections raises serious questions about motive.

It is also worth recalling that Ireland already has tools for international cooperation. As a signatory to the United Nations Convention on the Law of the Sea (UNCLOS), it participates in a framework that offers legal protections to submarine infrastructure and obligates nations to allow maintenance, not obstruction. If violations were to occur, diplomatic and legal paths would be available. NATO membership is not a precondition for invoking international support or asserting maritime rights.

Moreover, Ireland can build out its own coast guard and maritime intelligence. It can invest in satellite surveillance and work with allies on cable mapping and anomaly detection—civilian measures that would actually yield usable protection. Yet these options are rarely mentioned by those advocating for NATO. Their silence suggests a different goal: not cable security, but cultural and political alignment with the West's military architecture.

The argument's seductive simplicity aids this effort. Who could oppose defending the infrastructure that powers our daily lives? It is framed as responsible leadership, even inevitability. But such framing skips a vital question: If the cables were not there, would NATO still be proposed? The answer is almost certainly yes. The cables are not the reason—they are the excuse—the vehicle, not the destination.

The scale of this narrative operation becomes more obvious when we consider the broader context. Ireland is under increasing pressure from the United States and the European Union to "do more" in defense. These pressures have been steady but non-confrontational—until now. What changed? The war in Ukraine, the rise of China, and a growing sense in Brussels and Washington that Europe must close its gaps. Ireland, by virtue of its neutrality and geographic position, is perceived as one such gap.

Rather than admit to a desire to plug that hole, politicians are dressing it up in the language of infrastructure protection. Instead of saying, "We want Ireland in NATO because it's useful to us," the message is, "Ireland must join to defend its own cables." This inversion of motive is the hallmark of geopolitical narrative strategy: make the benefit to others look like a duty to yourself. It's how empires have always worked.

Let us also not forget that these cables are primarily economic infrastructure. They are not state secrets flowing from Dublin to

Washington—they are data pipelines filled with financial transactions, cloud backups, and Zoom calls. Yes, their disruption would be costly. But so would the loss of a power grid, airport hub, or seaport. No one is suggesting sending NATO troops to protect Cork Harbor. Why, then, are the cables singled out?

The answer lies in how they can be used, not how they might be damaged. By raising the spectre of threat, the state can justify surveillance powers, military spending, and diplomatic shifts that would otherwise be politically radioactive. The cables are useful precisely because they are both vital and invisible. Their value lies not just in what they transmit, but in what they allow to be transmitted politically.

As always, we must ask: who benefits from this? The answer is not the public. The average citizen gains no additional safety from military alliances that bring new obligations and risks. Nor does the small business that depends on stable internet. Nor does the student researching in Galway, or the retiree in Wexford. The beneficiaries are more remote: defense contractors, NATO bureaucrats, foreign embassies, and politicians who want to appear globally relevant.

The greatest danger, however, is what happens when these narratives succeed. Once neutrality is compromised, it is nearly impossible to retrieve. NATO does not offer part-time membership. There is no asterisk beside Article 5. Once Ireland enters, it joins a system of obligations that extend far beyond cable protection. A war in the Baltics, a cyberattack on a Polish server, or a skirmish in the Arctic—any of these could compel Irish involvement.

At that point, the question of cables will seem quaint. The discussion will have moved to troop commitments, military budgets, and alliance politics. And the public, having been told that it was all about infrastructure, may find itself wondering how it became all about war.

If the undersea cables are as important as the Irish government now insists, then one would expect a transparent, well-resourced national plan to protect them. But no such plan has been offered. There are no detailed government documents outlining the exact threat profile, no expert consultations published, no white papers proposing enhanced civilian infrastructure. Instead, the narrative leaps straight from danger to NATO, bypassing a host of other possibilities. This is not pragmatism. It is a deliberate narrowing of public perception, crafted to ensure that only one solution—military alignment—seems viable.

But Ireland does have other options. Many of them are grounded in existing law, infrastructure, and diplomatic traditions. These solutions deserve attention, not just as alternatives, but as preferable and proportionate responses to the actual risks involved.

First, the international legal framework already provides mechanisms for cable protection. The United Nations Convention on the Law of the Sea (UNCLOS) includes provisions that safeguard submarine cables from intentional damage and obligate states to allow their maintenance. Ireland is a signatory. If there are credible threats to these systems, Ireland can and should pursue stronger enforcement through diplomatic channels. Multilateral cooperation—especially with nearby nations that also host cable landings—is a powerful tool. It is how Europe built its cross-border electricity grids, its train networks, and its air traffic controls. Cables are no different.

Second, Ireland could invest in its own civilian infrastructure and monitoring capacity. Currently, the country's naval and coast guard resources are modest, underfunded, and in need of modernization. But these agencies, alongside telecommunications experts and cybersecurity analysts, could be tasked with overseeing cable routes, flagging unusual marine activity, and responding swiftly to interruptions. These aren't acts of war. They're acts of stewardship.

The country can also leverage its technological ecosystem. Ireland hosts dozens of global data centers and has direct relationships with tech giants that rely on cable infrastructure. A coordinated national task force—comprised of government, industry, and academia—could address redundancy, threat detection, and emergency protocols. Such a task force would be far more effective than an outsourcing strategy to foreign generals unfamiliar with the local topography or civil protocols.

Moreover, Ireland can work with cable operators themselves. Most cables are maintained by international consortia with vested interests in keeping traffic flowing smoothly. These companies already run fleet operations for cable laying and repair, have systems in place for rerouting data during outages, and frequently collaborate across borders. Ireland could request increased coverage in its nearby waters, co-fund a regional repair vessel, or negotiate shared monitoring agreements. All of this would enhance security—without requiring a single soldier.

Then there's the matter of resilience. Every modern infrastructure system depends not on the absence of failure, but on the ability to recover quickly. Internet infrastructure is no different. When a cable is cut—whether by accident or malice—data traffic is instantly rerouted. Multiple connections ensure that no single point of failure can cause catastrophic disruption. Ireland is already plugged into this global mesh. Strengthening its connectivity—by adding new cable routes, supporting satellite backup systems, or investing in edge computing—would do more to secure the nation than any NATO commitment could.

The rise of satellite-based alternatives only strengthens this point. Starlink, OneWeb, and other low-Earth orbit satellite networks are rapidly expanding their global reach. While not yet capable of replacing undersea cables for bulk traffic, they offer an invaluable form of redundancy. In 2022, when Tonga's only cable was severed by a volcanic eruption, satellites—not soldiers—restored emergency connectivity. NATO did not deploy warships. Civilian infrastructure did the job.

The potential for backup through satellite systems is growing. With the launch of high-bandwidth LEO satellites offering speeds comparable to fibre—and with latency decreasing year by year—these tools are becoming not just feasible, but essential. Combined with land-based routing through neighboring states, they create a system where outages are manageable, not catastrophic. A government that truly wanted to protect Ireland's digital infrastructure would be focused on these advancements, not military branding.

What's more, Ireland is perfectly positioned to lead in sustainable cable development. The global push for greener infrastructure is now reaching undersea systems. New cable deployments are being designed with lower power usage, more durable materials, and environmentally responsible routing. Ireland, with its renewable energy leadership and position at the edge of Europe, could be a test bed for next-generation systems—if it remains independent enough to chart its own course.

Contrast all of this with the NATO pitch. There are no proposals for NATO to fund new cables. There are no plans for NATO forces to conduct deep-sea repairs. There is no framework within the alliance to manage cable traffic or coordinate civilian redundancy. NATO is not a cable management agency. It is a military bloc designed for conflict scenarios. Its primary strength is conventional and nuclear deterrence, not cable protection. Aligning Ireland with NATO does not make cables safer. It simply makes them part of a larger geopolitical strategy.

It must also be said: militarizing cable protection creates new risks. Once these systems are linked to alliance strategies, they may be viewed as strategic targets. A cable used by a neutral Ireland is very different, in the eyes of a rival power, from one used by a NATO-aligned Ireland. Neutrality offers ambiguity, and in geopolitical terms, ambiguity can be protective. It says: we are not part of your conflict. Once that veil is lifted, so is the restraint that comes with it.

Indeed, NATO alignment might inadvertently increase the likelihood that Irish infrastructure becomes a pawn in future conflicts. Even if Ireland remains on the periphery of military operations, the mere fact of alliance can be enough to alter perceptions. In that sense, the supposed cure may introduce a new disease: strategic exposure.

In trying to "protect" a part of its infrastructure, Ireland may well be exposing its entire foreign policy to manipulation. The issue is no longer whether undersea cables are important—they are. The issue is whether we are being honest about what they require. They require cooperation, redundancy, innovation, and investment—not armed alliances.

At the core of the undersea cable argument lies a deeper democratic dilemma. Policy decisions of this magnitude—decisions about national alignment, military obligations, and the possible erosion of sovereignty—should only be made with the explicit, informed consent of the public. That consent must be based on open discourse, not manipulated by threat inflation or geopolitical sleight-of-hand. Yet what Ireland faces today is not an honest public debate about neutrality, but a campaign of implication, silence, and fear.

Neutrality is not a bureaucratic checkbox—it is a civic ideal. It is bound up in Ireland's post-colonial identity, its history of non-alignment, and its global reputation as a peace-oriented nation. To discard it should require more than policy briefs and strategic partnerships. It should demand referenda, public forums, parliamentary inquiry, and above all, a national conversation conducted in plain language.

But we are not being offered that. Instead, we are being given a story. A story of technological peril so complicated that only government experts can grasp it, so urgent that ordinary debate is too slow, and so uniquely dangerous that the only solution is foreign military integration. This narrative bypasses the public's ability to choose and replaces it with a manufactured sense of inevitability. It is not persuasion—it is conditioning.

Consider how the issue has been framed: first as a technical concern, then a strategic threat, and finally a moral imperative. Ireland is not merely advised to consider NATO—it is told that anything less would be irresponsible. This rhetorical escalation silences nuance. If one questions NATO membership, they are accused of ignoring the threat. If one defends neutrality, they are said to be stuck in the past. It is a classic strategy: make the present feel so exceptional that all principles must be suspended.

This is not the first time such framing has been used. In the post-9/11 world, many Western governments introduced sweeping security legislation by claiming that modern threats made old freedoms obsolete. Those freedoms have proven hard to recover. In this light, neutrality should not be viewed as a leftover from a simpler time—but as a check against panic-driven policymaking. It offers space for reflection, caution, and diplomacy. It gives Ireland a unique position in global affairs—one worth protecting.

And the public, when asked, tends to agree. Poll after poll shows strong support for neutrality. The idea that Ireland should not be involved in other nations' wars still resonates deeply, across political lines and generations. It is not just a foreign policy stance—it is an expression of national will. That is precisely why neutrality is being attacked not head-on, but from the side. The government knows it would struggle to win a referendum on NATO. So it changes the terms of the debate: don't talk about NATO, talk about cables. Don't talk about war, talk about infrastructure. Don't talk about neutrality, talk about security.

This sleight-of-hand is not merely dishonest—it is dangerous. If neutrality is to be revisited, let it be done with honesty and courage. Let the case be made openly, with facts, not shadows. Let the public decide whether to trade independence for alignment. Let us not sleepwalk into entanglement because someone said our internet might go down.

It is also worth noting how this strategy undermines institutional trust. In democratic societies, public faith in government is rooted in transparency. When leaders use fear to circumvent consent, that trust erodes. And once it is lost, it is hard to restore. Ireland cannot afford a future in which neutrality is abandoned and faith in government collapses in tandem.

But this erosion is already underway. The cable threat has become a catch-all justification, rolled out whenever critics question NATO involvement or expanded defense budgets. It has become a tool to silence dissent, to frame skepticism as recklessness. That framing is as corrosive to democratic dialogue as it is to policy integrity. If questioning military alignment is framed as disloyal, then democracy has already lost its compass.

So where does this leave us? It leaves us with a responsibility—to demand better. Better leadership. Better transparency. Better debate. It is not enough to argue for neutrality as a nostalgic virtue. It must be defended as a present necessity, rooted in logic and principle. And the burden of proof must fall not on those who wish to preserve it, but on those who seek to dismantle it.

If neutrality is outdated, then let that be proven in the open. If military alliances are necessary, let their case be made in daylight. Let us hear, in detail, what the threat is, what the alternatives are, what the obligations entail, and what the costs will be. Let us not be led by inference and implication, but by informed choice.

And let us remember that neutrality, once surrendered, cannot be easily reclaimed. Military alliances do not come with exit clauses that restore innocence. Once Ireland is part of a war plan, a command structure, or a logistical chain, it is in. And the next generation will live with that decision.

The truth is that cables do need protection—but so does democracy. Infrastructure can be repaired. Civil liberties, once corroded, take longer to rebuild. The integrity of a nation lies not in how quickly it joins the fight, but in how well it guards the right to choose when—and if—to fight at all.

Ireland's place on the western edge of Europe has always carried strategic weight. During World War II, that position gave Ireland leverage as a neutral actor. In the Cold War, it enabled quiet diplomacy. Today, it places the country at the center of transatlantic data flows. The cables that carry our emails, our banking transfers, our cloud storage, and our online meetings pass through Irish shores. But this strategic value does not necessitate strategic submission. On the contrary, it presents a unique opportunity—if we choose independence over alignment.

Neutrality has never meant indifference, isolation, or judgment. Ireland has long been a nation capable of saying "no" when others rush to say "yes." It has joined UN peacekeeping missions, brokered humanitarian efforts, and upheld multilateralism on its own terms. This is not weakness—it is wisdom, and it is increasingly rare.

The push to militarize cable protection undercuts that legacy. It tells us that neutrality is a relic, that independence is irresponsible, and that only the shield of a superpower can ensure our survival. But history tells a different story. Neutrality kept Ireland out of wars that ravaged its neighbors. It gave it the credibility to mediate and the space to grow economically. And it allowed the country to remain above the binary choices of East vs. West.

Today, that binary is being reasserted. As global tensions rise, especially between NATO and the emerging China-Russia axis, countries are once again being asked to choose sides. But choosing sides does not always mean choosing safety. Sometimes, it means choosing entrapment. A neutral Ireland can serve as a forum, a haven, a voice of reason. A militarized Ireland becomes a node in someone else's strategy.

To maintain this independence in a digital age, Ireland must take cable security seriously—but through its own lens. It must invest in civilian maritime protection, technical redundancy, and international regulation. It must support satellite backup and work with private tech giants to improve infrastructure. It must collaborate regionally, not capitulate globally.

And it must resist the creeping logic of inevitability. There is nothing inevitable about NATO membership. It is a choice. And like all choices of consequence, it must be made in full view of the facts and the people. Not under the fog of vague threat. Not beneath the weight of political expediency. But through collective will.

There are powerful forces that would benefit from Irish alignment—military contractors, foreign governments, and political elites seeking global credentials. But there are few clear benefits for the Irish public. Increased defense spending, reduced autonomy in foreign policy, and heightened risk of entanglement are all part of the package. These are not fringe fears. They are the real, documented obligations of membership.

And once the decision is made, it is difficult to reverse. NATO is not a revolving door. It is a commitment of shared defense and shared war. One cannot be a little bit neutral, just as one cannot be a little bit at war.

Perhaps the greatest irony is that the cables now being used to argue for militarization were laid under conditions of peace and neutrality. The tech firms that chose Ireland did so because it was stable, rule-based, and unaligned. To militarize that infrastructure is not to protect it—it is to change its nature. A Google data center under an Irish flag is one thing. A Google data center under a NATO flag is quite another.

There will always be threats. That is the nature of the world. But sovereignty is not about eliminating risk. It is about deciding how to face it. Do we do so as an independent nation? Or as a junior partner in a military bloc with its own agenda?

To those who claim that neutrality is no longer feasible, we say: prove it. Show the Irish people the facts, the risks, and the alternatives. Let the debate be held in public, not behind closed doors. Let the choice be made freely, not under pressure. And let us remember that being small is not the same as being weak. Ireland's strength has never come from its size—it has come from its clarity of purpose.

Let the undersea cables be protected. But let Irish neutrality still be protected more fiercely. For it is not just infrastructure that makes a country strong. It is values. It is independence. And it is the unshakable belief that security is not merely about what you join, but what you stand for.

11

NEUTRALITY IN THE FACE OF ECONOMIC COERCION

In April 2025, Ireland awoke to a changed economic reality. President Donald Trump, newly re-elected and emboldened, announced a sweeping global tariff regime branded "Liberation Day." In its crosshairs was Ireland—a neutral country with no military ties to NATO and no history of participation in foreign wars. Yet neutrality offered no immunity. The United States, Ireland's single largest trading partner, imposed a punitive 20% tariff on Irish exports across a broad spectrum of sectors. While the headlines focused on economic protectionism, the underlying message was strategic: those who benefit from U.S. markets but resist U.S. strategic alignment would no longer be shielded from consequence.

This development pierced the myth that neutrality, in an era of economic weaponization, could offer a sanctuary. Ireland, long praised for its open economy and diplomacy, was now a test case in 21st-century coercive statecraft. The country's trade-first model—built on low corporate taxes, regulatory predictability, and access to both the EU and U.S. markets—was suddenly vulnerable to unilateral disruption. What was being challenged was not only Ireland's economic structure, but its sovereign right to pursue a foreign policy that refused military entanglement.

While the effects of the tariffs were immediate and material—jobs lost, shipments delayed, investment frozen—the deeper impact was symbolic. Ireland had been designated expendable. The price of maintaining neutrality was no longer just diplomatic isolation; it now carried direct financial cost.

In the context of escalating global economic aggression, a new debate emerged in Dublin: could Ireland continue to afford neutrality, or would NATO membership offer a form of strategic shelter? Article 5 of the North Atlantic Treaty, which guarantees collective defense, had always been cited as the ultimate deterrent against military threats. But Ireland's predicament was not military. It was economic. The question now was whether NATO could offer protection not just from bullets and bombs, but from tariffs and economic siege.

The financial costs of NATO membership are significant. While not explicitly mandated, member states are expected to spend at least 2% of GDP on defense. Ireland currently spends approximately 0.3%. Achieving even half of NATO's target would require tripling defense allocations—an increase of over €3 billion annually. This would not include additional infrastructure upgrades, training, or integration into NATO command structures, nor the soft costs of political alignment and diplomatic positioning. In other words, joining NATO would be a multi-billion-euro commitment in a time of shrinking tax revenue and trade uncertainty.

Simultaneously, Ireland's corporate tax model—particularly the presence of American tech and pharmaceutical giants—was under siege. While the pharmaceutical sector had been temporarily spared from the initial wave of tariffs, there was no illusion in the Department of Finance that this would last. Secretary Howard Lutnick's public statements had made clear that intellectual property held in Ireland "for tax purposes" was an affront to U.S. economic interests. This meant that the economic foundation which had underwritten Ireland's fiscal independence for two decades was now politically vulnerable.

The contradiction is glaring: to join NATO is to incur a new, permanent financial burden in the billions, even as Ireland's existing tax base faces a slow-motion erosion by geopolitical pressure. Simply put, Ireland cannot afford to finance NATO while simultaneously withstanding coordinated economic sanctions from its largest export market.

Segment Three: The EU's Quiet Pressure and Ireland's Strategic Squeeze

While the U.S. deployed tariffs as a blunt instrument of coercion, the European Union applied subtler pressure. Ireland, as a member of the EU, has long benefited from access to the single market and regulatory protections, but this membership comes with increasing expectations—particularly regarding security and defense integration. Though the EU does not mandate NATO membership, the political current in Brussels is unmistakably flowing toward military coordination.

Participation in PESCO (Permanent Structured Cooperation), the European Defence Fund (EDF), and discussions around a more autonomous EU defense identity have put Ireland in a complicated position. While legally neutral, Ireland is now participating in structures that demand long-term defense spending commitments and harmonized procurement—often interoperable with NATO systems. The more Ireland integrates into EU defense frameworks, the harder it becomes to remain neutral in practice.

As detailed in Chapter 8, the Lisbon Treaty's mutual defense clause under Article 42.7 offers opt-outs for neutral states, and Ireland has availed of this. Yet funding instruments, access to defense research grants, and procurement mechanisms now increasingly favor those states that align closely with common defense goals. This form of financial favoritism acts as pressure by omission: a message that unless Ireland steps further into the defense bloc, its influence—and funding—will diminish.

Economically, this adds another layer of vulnerability. Not only is Ireland being punished by the U.S. for neutrality, but it risks being marginalized within the EU for the same stance. In trade terms, Ireland is too aligned with Europe to chart an independent path, yet too vulnerable to U.S. pressure to resist American aggression alone. Neutrality, once a source of flexibility, is becoming an economic fault line.

This strategic squeeze—caught between U.S. coercion and EU conditionality—has revealed how neutrality, in the modern global economy, requires more than principle. It requires preparedness.

In response to the unprecedented convergence of economic threats, Irish policymakers began advancing a new framework: the National Economic Intelligence and Recovery Unit (NEIRU). Proposed as a dedicated government body, NEIRU would serve as Ireland's frontline defense against economic coercion. Unlike traditional trade policy institutions, its mandate would be broader—covering corporate behavior analysis, industrial protection planning, and supply chain resilience.

NEIRU would function in real time, identifying which sectors are vulnerable to foreign pressure and preparing contingency plans for sudden capital flight or disinvestment. For example, if a pharmaceutical company in Cork threatened to relocate production due to U.S. tariffs or pressure from Washington to repatriate IP, NEIRU would have the legal and financial tools to intervene. This could involve temporary state ownership, strategic retooling, or redirecting production toward non-U.S. markets.

Importantly, NEIRU is not a protectionist tool. It is an autonomy safeguard. It is designed to ensure that Ireland can remain a competitive and independent economy even when faced with foreign economic aggression—be it through tariffs, sanctions, or reputational attacks. As NEIRU matures, it could also serve as an early warning system for trade disputes, allowing Ireland to anticipate rather than react to threats.

The principle here is simple: neutrality must be defended economically just as it is defended diplomatically. Military neutrality in a world of weaponized trade is meaningless if a country cannot protect the infrastructure and industries that fund its sovereignty.

Segment Five: Reclaiming the Narrative – The Fight Against the "Tax Scam" Myth

Amid the material damage inflicted by tariffs and investment freezes, another front in the battle for Ireland's economic sovereignty has emerged: narrative warfare. The U.S. administration's rhetoric around Ireland as a "tax scam" has become a powerful, corrosive tool. Repeated in speeches, cable news soundbites, and campaign rallies, the phrase has transformed from accusation into strategy. It is a calculated political weapon, designed to vilify Ireland's tax regime in the court of public opinion—especially among Irish-American voters—and to justify punitive trade policies under the guise of economic justice.

This portrayal, however, is detached from fact. Ireland's 12.5% corporate tax rate has been a fixed and publicly debated cornerstone of national policy for over two decades. It was never secretive, nor imposed unilaterally; it has been fully vetted under the OECD's BEPS (Base Erosion and Profit Shifting) framework and was incorporated into the G20's agreement on a global minimum tax. Ireland has been a proactive, transparent participant in international tax reform discussions, not an outlier or rogue actor.

And yet, perception trumps legality in geopolitics. The tax scam myth is powerful precisely because it resonates emotionally. It recasts Ireland from economic partner to opportunist, presenting its success as parasitic rather than earned. The real aim is not tax fairness, but power reallocation—pressuring U.S. multinationals to onshore jobs and assets, not through reform or competition, but through coercion.

Ireland cannot ignore this narrative front. It must be countered with facts—but also with emotion, dignity, and national pride. The government must reframe the story: Ireland is not stealing prosperity from America; it has been a stable partner, offering skilled labor, legal certainty, and access to the EU for U.S. companies. Those investments have benefitted both sides, and attempts to undermine them will cause mutual harm—not just for Ireland, but for U.S. workers, shareholders, and consumers.

Efforts to reclaim this narrative must extend beyond policy briefings. Ireland's embassies, diaspora networks, and cultural institutions must engage directly with Irish-American communities, business councils, and legislators. Ireland's story—its rise from poverty to prosperity through hard work, innovation, and responsible governance—must be told loudly and often. In a world where narratives shape policy, silence is complicity.

The structural lesson of 2025 is clear: no small country can afford to be dependent on a single superpower. Ireland's overreliance on the U.S. for exports, tax revenue, and corporate employment has exposed it to disproportionate risk. If Ireland's neutrality is to survive in the modern world, it must be supported by a diversified economic portfolio. That means not just signing trade agreements, but building deep, mutually beneficial partnerships beyond the Atlantic.

The government's proposed Export Diversification Strategy is a step in this direction. It envisions targeted expansion into Asia, the Middle East, and Africa—regions with rising consumer demand and a hunger for premium goods and services. Irish dairy and whiskey producers are already exploring markets in India and Japan. Biopharma executives have opened trade dialogues with South Korea and Singapore. But more is needed. Logistics infrastructure must be upgraded. Export financing schemes expanded. Cultural exchange and language programs embedded into trade missions. Diplomacy must become economic diplomacy.

Domestically, this rebalancing requires a shift in focus: away from attracting foreign direct investment as the only growth engine and toward empowering Irish-owned firms. These firms are less likely to relocate when geopolitical winds change. They are more embedded in the national fabric and contribute to local economic stability. Strategic support for homegrown companies—in green tech, AI, biomedicine, and agritech—must now become a national priority. That support should include tax incentives, public-private R&D partnerships, and state-backed venture capital.

The new economic neutrality must be defined not by withdrawal from global trade, but by resilience within it. It is not about turning inward, but about standing on two feet—able to trade with all, dependent on none. This principle is the only path to sustainable sovereignty in a century where markets, like militaries, are increasingly instruments of control.

Ireland's economic balancing act—between European political integration and American investment dependence—has become increasingly untenable. With one bloc demanding solidarity and the other using its power to punish, Ireland's traditional role as a bridge is being challenged. The two-tier tariff structure imposed by the U.S., where Northern Ireland enjoys a 10% rate while the Republic faces 20%, is a prime example of how geopolitics is now shaping domestic economics. While the split may appear benign, its implications are not. It risks reopening political fissures on the island, undermining the economic integration that has underpinned peace since the Good Friday Agreement.

Ireland's vulnerability in this new order is not the result of bad choices. It is the consequence of success: becoming a globalized, rules-based, open economy in a world where those very principles are under assault. The EU's planned countermeasures to the U.S. tariffs could deepen Ireland's exposure, hitting American firms based in Dublin and Cork while offering few direct benefits. Ireland must advocate for differentiated policies within Brussels—mechanisms that acknowledge the disproportionate pain borne by smaller, open economies in the line of fire.

At the same time, Ireland must define the terms of its neutrality. It cannot be a policy of abstention or moral distance. It must be a proactive doctrine of independence—one that includes the economic tools and strategic foresight to navigate a fractured world. In this context, neutrality is not a relic. It is a platform. A mode of leadership. A declaration that Ireland will not be a pawn in the power games of larger states, but a principled actor willing to assert its right to chart its own course.

The lessons of 2025 are sobering. Ireland has learned that economic vulnerability can be exploited just as surely as military weakness. Tariffs can hit harder than tanks. Political slurs, if repeated long enough, can do as much damage as sanctions. And neutrality—when left unguarded—can become a target rather than a shield.

At the heart of this crisis is a legal and constitutional reckoning. While neutrality is not explicitly enshrined in Bunreacht na hÉireann, Article 29 reaffirms Ireland's sovereignty in foreign affairs and its commitment to international peace. Economic coercion, used to extract geopolitical concessions, is a violation of those principles. It demands a constitutional response that aligns economic independence with the broader doctrine of neutrality.

Could Ireland legally join NATO in this context? Yes. But could it afford to? That answer is far less clear. The costs—fiscal, reputational, strategic—would be immense. As previous chapters explored, NATO membership would commit Ireland to sustained defense spending, operational deployment expectations, and the loss of diplomatic independence in matters of war and peace. Overlay this with a shrinking tax base, tariff threats, and capital flight, and the argument becomes one not of security, but of survival.

Neutrality must now be understood in economic terms. It is no longer enough to stay out of military alliances. Ireland must also stay out of coercive alignments that compromise its ability to make independent decisions in its national interest. This means asserting its economic identity with the same resolve it once applied to its diplomatic positioning.

The creation of a National Economic Intelligence and Recovery Unit is not a panacea, but it is a beginning. So too is the Export Diversification

Strategy. These are not reactions—they are declarations: that Ireland intends to defend its neutrality with strategy, not slogans.

In doing so, Ireland will not stand alone. Other small nations—Finland, Switzerland, Singapore, Costa Rica—face similar pressures. Ireland can lead by example, building coalitions for fair trade, rules-based governance, and economic justice. That leadership begins by rejecting the false choice between compliance and collapse. Ireland has the right to define its own future—and the responsibility to defend that right with clarity, conviction, and courage.

Neutrality, then, is not a retreat. It is a position. One that says Ireland will engage with the world on its own terms—not from fear, but from principle.

And in a world where sovereignty is increasingly for sale, that principle is priceless.

12

GREENLAND ABANDONED
WHAT IT MEANS FOR IRELAND

Greenland, with its vast icy expanse and sparse population, has long been treated as a distant curiosity in international affairs. Yet as the Arctic melts and global powers turn their eyes northward, its strategic importance has become impossible to ignore. Beneath Greenland's glaciers lie rare earth minerals essential for modern technologies, while its position makes it a linchpin for control over emerging Arctic shipping lanes. The United States, in particular, has identified Greenland as a critical asset in its broader geopolitical strategy.

Recent years have already hinted at increasing American interest in Greenland, notably when President Donald Trump publicly suggested buying it from Denmark in 2019. At the time, the idea was dismissed as a diplomatic misstep, but it revealed an undercurrent of U.S. strategic thought. The Arctic, and Greenland specifically, are no longer viewed merely as distant territories but as key frontiers in the competition for global influence. If future geopolitical pressures align with leadership in Washington willing to act decisively, a scenario in which the U.S. exerts significant control over Greenland becomes increasingly plausible.

Should a future American administration seek to expand its influence, the approach is unlikely to be overtly aggressive. Rather than a military occupation, such a move would probably unfold through economic investments, increased military cooperation under existing treaties, and support for Greenlandic autonomy. The groundwork has already been laid, with U.S. military presence at Thule Air Base and growing interest in Arctic security. Economic aid, promises of infrastructure development, and strategic partnerships could serve as tools to shift Greenland closer to Washington and further from Copenhagen.

Denmark, while retaining sovereignty over Greenland, may find its position increasingly challenged, especially if Greenlandic political forces begin to favour deeper ties with the U.S. in exchange for economic benefits. This shift could strain Denmark's ability to maintain full authority, particularly if American support emboldens autonomy movements within Greenland. In such a scenario, Denmark might appeal to NATO or the EU for support, expecting solidarity against external pressure. However, the likelihood of a robust response from these alliances is uncertain, especially if the pressure comes from within their own ranks.

This potential future raises troubling questions about the reliability of collective defense arrangements. NATO's mutual defense clause, Article 5, is often cited as a guarantee of support, but it is fundamentally dependent on political will. If the perceived aggressor is the United States, the alliance's ability to act may be severely compromised. Similarly, the European Union, lacking a unified defense structure, may find itself diplomatically paralyzed, unwilling to jeopardize transatlantic relations over Greenland.

For Ireland, this scenario serves as a cautionary tale. A small, neutral nation watching from the sidelines, Ireland must consider what Greenland's predicament could imply for its own security. If a close NATO ally like Denmark can be left isolated, what assurances does Ireland have, especially as a non-aligned state? The lesson is not just about Greenland but about the fragility of promises made by alliances that are ultimately governed by the interests of their most powerful members.

Ireland's strategic location, like Greenland's, places it within the sphere of interest of larger powers. The country's airspace, maritime territory, and data infrastructure are vital links in global systems, making it a potential focal point in any future geopolitical contest. If larger nations sought to use Irish territory or infrastructure for their own purposes, would Ireland's sovereignty be respected? The past offers little comfort. The use of Shannon Airport by U.S. forces, often without full transparency, suggests that even now, Ireland's neutrality can be undermined when it suits more powerful partners.

In light of these possibilities, Ireland must carefully evaluate its position. Joining military alliances like NATO may appear to offer security, but as the potential scenario in Greenland suggests, such security is conditional. It depends on the interests of the dominant powers, and when those interests conflict with the rights of smaller states, history shows that the latter often come second.

Neutrality, therefore, should not be seen as a weakness but as a strategic choice that allows Ireland to maintain control over its foreign policy and national defense. However, neutrality must be backed by preparedness. Ireland cannot afford to rely solely on diplomatic goodwill. It must invest in the capability to defend its sovereignty across multiple domains, including cyber, economic, and maritime security.

The Greenland scenario, while hypothetical, is rooted in current trends. The Arctic is becoming a contested space, and Greenland's role in that contest will only grow. If the U.S. does seek to expand its influence there, the precedent set could embolden similar actions elsewhere. Ireland must prepare for a world where power is increasingly asserted through non-military means—economic pressure, political influence, and technological dominance.

This potential future serves as a call for Ireland to strengthen its neutrality, not abandon it. By reinforcing its sovereignty, diversifying its economic relationships, and developing independent defense capabilities, Ireland can position itself to resist external pressures, regardless of where they originate. The security of small nations in the 21st century will depend not on promises from alliances but on their ability to maintain independence in an increasingly multipolar world.

As global power dynamics evolve, Greenland is positioned at the intersection of economic ambition and strategic necessity, not just for the United States, but for other powers interested in the Arctic. The gradual melting of polar ice is opening new maritime routes and exposing rich deposits of critical minerals, which are becoming increasingly valuable as nations transition to advanced technologies and seek alternatives to traditional supply chains dominated by China. Greenland's role in this emerging landscape makes it an irresistible prospect for any state with aspirations to control the Arctic's future.

Denmark's capacity to defend its authority over Greenland is not limitless. Though it retains formal sovereignty, the day-to-day realities of governance in Greenland are shaped by its increasing autonomy. If Greenland's leadership sees more opportunity in aligning with U.S. strategic and economic interests, a shift in allegiance could occur gradually and legally, rather than through open conflict. This would place Denmark in a difficult position—facing a legal and political challenge, rather than a military one. NATO, structured to address military threats, might have little to offer in terms of support.

In such a scenario, the U.S. could maintain that its involvement is fully in line with Greenlandic self-determination, emphasizing development aid and defense cooperation under the guise of mutual benefit. These developments, while technically respecting legal frameworks, could effectively sideline Denmark and lead to a de facto shift in Greenland's alignment. The rest of NATO might regard this as a matter of internal adjustment between allies rather than a violation warranting intervention.

Ireland, observing this from its position of neutrality, would need to assess what such shifts in alliance dynamics imply for its own security environment. If NATO, in this plausible future, cannot or will not act to uphold the sovereign claims of one of its own founding members due to internal power dynamics, then what assurance could Ireland find in any similar arrangement? The political reality is that alliances, though framed as partnerships of equals, often operate on a hierarchy of interests. Smaller states are expected to align with the priorities of larger powers, and when they do not, their concerns may be dismissed or overridden.

Ireland's historical experience provides context for such concerns. Throughout its past, the country has faced external pressures from larger powers seeking to influence its internal affairs. While in the modern era these pressures are more likely to come through economic or diplomatic channels than military ones, they are no less real. The precedent of Greenland, should such a scenario unfold, would serve as a stark reminder that sovereignty must be actively protected, not just asserted.

This understanding should inform Ireland's approach to neutrality in the coming years. Rather than viewing neutrality as a passive stance, Ireland must invest in making it a credible and resilient position. This involves developing capacities that allow the country to detect and respond to threats that fall below the threshold of conventional warfare. It also requires building diplomatic relationships that respect Ireland's non-aligned status and that support multilateral approaches to security and conflict resolution.

Ireland's strategic location and its role in global data and financial systems mean that it cannot afford to neglect the realities of hybrid threats. Cybersecurity, for instance, must become a national priority, with robust systems to protect critical infrastructure and data networks from foreign interference. Similarly, economic resilience must be strengthened to reduce the leverage that any one country might have over Irish decision-making. Diversifying trade relationships, encouraging domestic innovation, and safeguarding key sectors from foreign control are all essential steps in this direction.

The potential scenario in Greenland also highlights the need for vigilance against political interference. Ireland's political and media landscape must be protected from foreign influence that seeks to shape public opinion or policy outcomes in ways that undermine sovereignty. Transparency in political financing, strong regulatory frameworks for lobbying, and public awareness campaigns are necessary tools to ensure that Ireland's democratic processes remain free from coercion.

In this emerging world, sovereignty is as much about internal coherence and resilience as it is about external defense. Ireland must therefore cultivate a sense of national purpose that is grounded in an understanding of the complexities of modern power. Neutrality, in this context, is not isolation but strategic engagement on Ireland's own terms. It is a commitment to peace and diplomacy, supported by the capacity to withstand pressures from all directions.

The scenario involving Greenland serves as a potential model for how the balance of power might shift in subtle but profound ways. It demonstrates how a small territory can become the focal point of great power competition, and how alliances may falter when confronted with internal contradictions. Ireland must learn from this, preparing itself not for the wars of the past, but for the contests of influence, control, and sovereignty that define the present and will shape the future.

In a world where alliances like NATO might fail to act decisively to protect smaller states from internal pressures exerted by dominant members, Ireland must recognize that its security lies in its own hands. It must adapt its national policies to reflect a new understanding of power—one that includes cyber influence, economic dependency, and information manipulation as tools of coercion just as potent as traditional military force.

For neutrality to remain a viable and respected position, Ireland must anchor it in the strongest possible legal and political foundations. Codifying neutrality within its Constitution would serve not only as a domestic safeguard against shifts in government policy but also as a clear signal internationally that Ireland's stance is firm and enduring. Such a constitutional commitment would elevate neutrality beyond the realm of policy debate, making it a core aspect of national identity.

Ireland's foreign policy must evolve to support this commitment. Rather than being reactive to the demands of larger blocs, Ireland should take a proactive role in international diplomacy, positioning itself as a leader among non-aligned nations. By engaging with other neutral or non-aligned states, Ireland can build a coalition that supports peaceful resolution of conflicts and resists the normalization of power politics that disregard the sovereignty of smaller nations.

Defense policy must also be reconsidered, not in terms of aligning with military blocs, but in terms of self-sufficiency. Ireland must enhance its maritime and airspace surveillance capabilities, ensuring that it can monitor and respond to any incursions into its territory. This does not mean expanding the military for offensive purposes, but rather building a credible defensive posture that deters violations of sovereignty.

Cybersecurity presents perhaps the most immediate challenge. As a hub for global technology firms and a key node in the transatlantic data network, Ireland is exposed to cyber threats that could undermine not only its economy but also its national security. Investment in cyber defense infrastructure, training of specialized personnel, and cooperation with other neutral nations on cyber intelligence will be critical. Ireland must be able to detect, deter, and respond to cyber threats without relying on military alliances whose interests may not align with its own.

Economic policy must also support strategic independence. Ireland should pursue a more balanced approach to foreign investment, ensuring that critical infrastructure remains under national control and that economic policy is not overly dependent on any one nation or bloc. Diversification of trade and investment partners, development of indigenous industries, and strategic management of natural and technological resources are essential to maintaining economic sovereignty.

Furthermore, Ireland must be prepared to resist political interference. This means not only ensuring that its own political processes are secure but also that its media and public discourse are resilient against manipulation.

Transparency in political financing, strong regulations on foreign lobbying, and public education on the risks of disinformation are necessary to safeguard democracy.

Ireland's global engagement should reflect its commitment to neutrality and peace. By playing an active role in international organizations focused on human rights, conflict resolution, and sustainable development, Ireland can reinforce its identity as a principled nation committed to global stability. This approach not only enhances Ireland's reputation but also builds alliances based on shared values rather than strategic expediency.

As power becomes increasingly diffuse, the ability of small nations to navigate the complexities of international relations will depend on their capacity to adapt and to stand firm in their principles. Ireland's history, marked by a struggle for independence and a commitment to self-determination, provides a strong foundation for such an approach. By learning from the potential scenario involving Greenland, Ireland can anticipate challenges and take steps now to ensure that it remains the master of its own destiny.

The future is uncertain, but Ireland's path need not be. Through thoughtful policy, strategic investment, and unwavering commitment to neutrality and sovereignty, Ireland can not only survive but thrive in a world where alliances are no longer reliable shields, and where independence, carefully guarded, becomes the true guarantor of security.

To conclude, the scenario unfolding around Greenland—still speculative, yet increasingly plausible—offers a profound insight into the evolving nature of international relations. It challenges the assumption that alliances, however long-standing or deeply institutionalized, provide unshakeable guarantees for smaller nations. The potential abandonment of Denmark in its stewardship over Greenland, under the pressure of an assertive United States acting in pursuit of strategic interests, highlights the fragility of such arrangements. For Ireland, this serves not as a distant cautionary tale but as a direct signal that in the shifting tides of global politics, the only reliable safeguard is a nation's own preparation and resolve.

Ireland stands at a crossroads where it must decide whether to deepen entanglements with alliances that may not respect its sovereignty or to reinforce a path of independent neutrality. This neutrality is not simply the absence of military engagement; it is a deliberate and proactive strategy, shaped by history and necessity, that positions Ireland as a nation committed to peace, diplomacy, and self-determination.

The betrayal of Denmark in this plausible future should awaken Ireland to the limitations of depending on others for defense and political support. While alliances can provide benefits, they are fundamentally instruments of convenience for their most powerful members. When the interests of these members diverge from those of smaller states, the latter often find themselves sidelined. Ireland must not allow itself to be placed in such a vulnerable position.

Strategic independence requires more than rhetorical commitments. It necessitates a comprehensive approach to national security, one that includes robust defense capabilities tailored to the realities of modern threats, a resilient economy that minimizes dependency, and a vigilant civil society that can resist external manipulation. Ireland must ensure that its critical infrastructure—digital, maritime, and financial—is secure from both overt and covert pressures. It must invest in technologies and institutions that support its autonomy and enable it to respond flexibly and effectively to emerging challenges.

The path forward also involves cultivating a strong and consistent diplomatic voice. Ireland has the opportunity to lead by example, demonstrating that a small nation can wield significant influence through moral authority and steadfast adherence to international law. By championing causes such as nuclear disarmament, human rights, and climate action, Ireland can build alliances of principle rather than convenience, reinforcing its standing on the global stage.

Domestically, a renewed commitment to neutrality should be enshrined in the nation's highest laws, ensuring that no future government can easily alter this foundational aspect of Irish identity. Public discourse must be informed by a clear understanding of what neutrality means in the contemporary world—a commitment not to isolation, but to sovereign decision-making and principled engagement.

The scenario with Greenland, whether it fully materializes or not, serves as a wake-up call. It illustrates how quickly the ground can shift beneath small nations when larger powers pursue their own agendas. Ireland must respond not with fear, but with a firm dedication to fortifying its independence. This does not mean rejecting all forms of international cooperation, but rather choosing carefully and deliberately the terms on which it engages with the world.

As the global order becomes more fragmented and unpredictable, Ireland has a unique chance to carve out a role as a beacon of neutrality and integrity. By preparing for a future where alliances may falter, Ireland secures not only its own sovereignty but also contributes to a more balanced and just international system.

The question is no longer whether Ireland should prepare for such a future, but whether it will act in time. The responsibility lies not with external forces, but within. Ireland must now ask itself whether it will follow the uncertain promises of others or lead with its own unwavering commitment to sovereignty. The choice is clear. The time to act is now.

13

WILL NATO MEMBERSHIP DETER FOREIGN INVESTMENT?

Ireland's transformation from a struggling economy into a global innovation hub is a well-documented success story. At the center of this transformation has been the country's strategic commitment to neutrality—an often overlooked but critical asset. While tax policy, education, and regulatory alignment with the EU have all played major roles, it is Ireland's political stability and military neutrality that have distinguished it from other European investment destinations. These twin attributes have consistently reassured global investors that Ireland is insulated from the political volatility and military entanglements that can threaten long-term operations and capital deployment.

For multinational firms, neutrality equals predictability. Ireland's non-aligned status has made it a safe bet for companies looking to house data centers, develop intellectual property, and operate complex supply chains.

While favorable tax conditions may have opened the door, it is Ireland's stable governance and neutral geopolitical stance that have convinced tech giants like Apple, Google, and Meta—and pharmaceutical leaders like Pfizer, MSD, and Johnson & Johnson—to put down roots. Stability attracts infrastructure; neutrality protects it.

This logic is not abstract. Tech and pharmaceutical companies, more than most, rely on continuity. Disruptions from war, sanctions, or unpredictable foreign policy shifts can paralyze operations. Ireland has avoided those shocks. That freedom from alignment has allowed it to become a European base for operations with global scope. NATO membership, by contrast, introduces a new layer of risk—legal, reputational, and strategic.

The calculus behind FDI is complex, but it is built on a simple premise: companies invest where risk is minimized. Political neutrality—especially in small, open economies—offers insulation from conflict, a safeguard against being drawn into sanctions regimes, and a buffer against reputational volatility. Ireland has benefited from this positioning, especially during periods of global instability. While other countries have had to navigate diplomatic backlashes or military alliances, Ireland has remained focused on growth, talent, and innovation.

By contrast, NATO membership would signal a decisive geopolitical realignment. Investors, particularly those from non-NATO countries like China, the UAE, or Singapore, could interpret that shift as a pivot away from neutral engagement and toward bloc-based politics. For global corporations with diverse investor bases and markets in both the West and the East, such a move may trigger boardroom reconsiderations.

The risk is not only geopolitical. NATO membership would also bring about expectations of increased defense spending. As noted in Chapter 6, member states are expected to allocate 2% of GDP toward defense. Ireland's current expenditure is roughly 0.3%. Meeting NATO benchmarks would require significant budgetary restructuring—likely pulling resources from infrastructure, education, and innovation programs that have underpinned investor confidence. That's not a cost easily absorbed by an economy that relies heavily on maintaining its business-friendly image.

Other countries offer clear lessons. Switzerland and Austria have maintained their neutrality and enjoyed steady flows of foreign investment over decades. Switzerland, for instance, is not in NATO or the EU, yet remains one of the world's most attractive environments for multinational banks, pharma giants, and advanced manufacturers. Austria, despite being an EU member, has resisted calls to militarize its foreign policy and continues to cultivate its status as a neutral, diplomatic actor. Both countries are seen as safe havens for long-term investment, not in spite of their neutrality, but because of it.

Conversely, countries like Finland and Sweden—recent NATO entrants—are now recalibrating their economies to accommodate military obligations. Their security is arguably enhanced, but the trade-offs are visible: increased defense budgets, new procurement structures, and shifting investor sentiment as global firms reassess exposure to military infrastructure. Ireland must examine whether the potential gains of collective defense outweigh the real-world economic price of losing its neutrality. The comparison is especially relevant for Ireland's pharmaceutical and data center industries. Both sectors demand geopolitical insulation. Both rely on uninterrupted access to markets, protection from cyber conflict, and reputational neutrality.

If Ireland ceases to be seen as an apolitical European hub, companies might begin to explore alternatives—perhaps within the EU's neutral fringes, or even outside Europe entirely.

While Ireland's U.S.-centric tax model and trade links are well known, less discussed is the growing role of non-Western investment in sectors such as green energy, fintech, and logistics. Sovereign wealth funds from the Middle East, private equity from Asia, and emerging-market tech investors have increasingly seen Ireland as a trusted neutral gateway to the EU. These partners do not see NATO membership as a security guarantee—they see it as a risk. China, despite geopolitical friction with the West, has shown sustained interest in European logistics, green energy, and data infrastructure. While Ireland has not embraced China to the same extent as some southern EU states, its neutrality has ensured diplomatic goodwill and investment access. NATO membership could damage this balance, especially given that NATO increasingly frames China as a strategic challenge. Likewise, the Gulf states have directed investments toward neutral European countries, using them as safe testing grounds for innovation projects, fintech pilots, and sustainable development ventures. Ireland's tech-savvy workforce, progressive business environment, and stable politics have made it a natural partner. Militarization, or even the perception of partisanship, could disrupt this trust.

NATO's utility is not in question for countries on the frontline of military risk. But Ireland is not on that frontier. Its value lies in being a strategic outlier—aligned economically, but not entangled militarily. That posture has made it a uniquely attractive base for cross-border capital. To compromise it for hypothetical security gains is to misunderstand what Ireland offers the world.

One of the most critical but underdiscussed risks of NATO membership is fiscal reallocation. Defense spending does not exist in a vacuum; it competes directly with other national priorities. Ireland's social and economic model has been fueled not only by low corporate taxes and a well-educated workforce, but by heavy investment in public infrastructure, digital innovation, education, and R&D incentives. These are precisely the areas that investors—from pharma labs to hyperscale data centers—rely on for long-term planning and execution.

Were Ireland to join NATO, it would face immense pressure to shift billions toward defense commitments. That would not only mean new costs for military procurement and strategic infrastructure—it would also almost certainly reduce state investment in the very services and programs that keep Ireland competitive. Investors would not see this as progress—they would see it as strategic drift.

Worse still, this shift may not deliver tangible domestic benefits. Ireland is unlikely to wield meaningful influence in NATO's strategic decision-making. As explored in earlier chapters, it would contribute economically and logistically but remain on the sidelines when operational decisions are made by the alliance's major powers. Ireland would lose neutrality—and control—without gaining sovereignty or security guarantees in return.

The result could be a chilling effect on future investment. While some NATO-aligned firms might be reassured, many others, particularly those prioritizing political neutrality and operational continuity, would reassess. Any perception that Ireland could become entangled in a military confrontation or subject to geopolitical retaliation—cyber or otherwise—would erode the confidence that has built Ireland's global profile.

Foreign investors may not be vocal about it, but their preferences are clear. They want regulatory clarity, diplomatic neutrality, and a commitment to long-term policy stability. They do not want risk. They do not want unpredictability. And they do not want to watch the country that has served as Europe's economic lighthouse turn itself into a forward operating post.

As Ireland faces mounting questions about its future security posture, it must confront one of the most important economic realities of its modern era: neutrality has been an asset, not a liability. It has made Ireland attractive not just for what it avoids—military entanglements and sanctions—but for what it offers: continuity, calm, and commitment to peaceful global engagement. While the NATO debate is often framed around defense obligations and military readiness, its economic implications are equally consequential. In earlier chapters we explored the risks of U.S. economic coercion and the fragility of relying too heavily on one trade partner. This chapter builds on that by showing that NATO membership could not only increase financial exposure—it could fundamentally undermine the logic that has made Ireland a magnet for multinational investment. Big Tech and pharmaceutical companies do not choose Ireland because it is a fortress—they choose it because it is an island of predictability in an increasingly unstable world. Their operations—data centers, R&D hubs, production lines—are high-capital, low-risk ventures that depend on long-term infrastructure and legal reliability. Ireland's neutrality is not incidental to that calculus; it is integral. Legal frameworks also matter. Ireland's neutrality is not just political tradition—it reflects Article 29 of the Irish Constitution, which commits the country to the pacific settlement of disputes and cooperation through international institutions. To abandon this posture without a constitutional review or public referendum would risk both political backlash and investor uncertainty. Neutrality is not the absence of alliances—it is the preservation of independence. NATO may offer collective defense, but it also limits individual discretion. For Ireland, a small but sophisticated economy that thrives on openness and agility, neutrality remains the policy best aligned with long-term prosperity. Foreign investors are watching—not just what Ireland does, but what it signals. A move toward NATO would send a message that Ireland is preparing for confrontation, not partnership. It would suggest that Ireland no longer sees neutrality as strength. That message, once sent, cannot be unsent. And the consequences may not come in missiles or troop deployments, but in missed investments, cancelled expansions, and redirected capital. If Ireland wishes to remain the world's most trusted node for innovation, commerce, and cross-border cooperation, it must defend its neutrality not as a relic, but as a strategic asset.

In the world of global capital, neutrality is more than a foreign policy—it is a business model. And it works.

14

THE IRISH NEUTRALITY AND SOVEREIGNTY ACT

Irish neutrality is more than a diplomatic tradition—it is a declaration of national character, rooted in sovereignty, independence, and a moral rejection of militarism. And yet, despite its centrality to Irish identity and foreign policy, neutrality remains absent from the Constitution of Ireland. This silence has become a liability.

From World War II to the Cold War, and through Ireland's EU membership and engagement with NATO's Partnership for Peace, neutrality has endured—but often only as a matter of policy. That policy has been vulnerable to executive discretion, foreign pressure, and incremental erosion. In recent years, Ireland has participated in EU defence initiatives such as PESCO, permitted military stopovers at Shannon Airport, and deepened informal ties with NATO—without any constitutional mandate or public consent.

The proposed Irish Neutrality and Sovereignty Act addresses this fragility. It calls for the enshrinement of neutrality in the Constitution (Bunreacht na hÉireann) and provides the legal, political, and institutional structures to make that neutrality enduring, enforceable, and democratically legitimate.

At its core, this Act would embed a commitment that Ireland shall remain a militarily neutral state. It would prohibit participation in military alliances, prevent automatic commitments to collective defence actions, and ban the hosting of foreign military bases or offensive infrastructure. Exceptions would exist only for UN-mandated peacekeeping missions or humanitarian interventions approved under the Triple Lock system—requiring the support of the Government, the Dáil Éireann, and a UN resolution.

Codifying neutrality would align Ireland's laws with the values long held by its people—and safeguard the nation from geopolitical currents it cannot control.

A constitutional commitment without legal enforcement is a paper shield. To ensure that Irish neutrality is more than a moral ideal, the Act proposes a clear and enforceable set of criminal penalties for public officials, institutions, or private entities that knowingly or negligently undermine the State's neutral status.

At the heart of this legal architecture is the principle of sovereignty through accountability.

The Act would criminalise:
- Secret commitments to foreign military alliances or intelligence-sharing pacts not approved by the Oireachtas;

- The establishment or permitting of foreign military bases, staging areas, or logistical support structures on Irish soil;
- Covert funding or support for joint arms procurement, research, or production under EU or NATO auspices;
- The use of Irish civilian infrastructure (airports, ports, data centers) for foreign military operations without explicit parliamentary approval and full public disclosure.

These offences would be tried under the jurisdiction of the High Court, and carry penalties ranging from fines and civil liability to imprisonment for up to ten years, depending on the severity and intent of the breach.

To protect against political misuse or procedural ambiguity, the Act establishes a legal presumption of neutrality, placing the burden on the State to justify any deviation under international humanitarian law or explicit constitutional exception. If neutrality is to be breached in exceptional cases, it must be openly declared, legally authorised, and subject to judicial review.

Additionally, whistleblower protections will be expanded under the Act to encourage civil servants, defence officials, and contractors to report violations of the neutrality framework. Any deliberate concealment of unconstitutional defence arrangements will itself constitute a criminal act.

As stated in previous segments, especially in the section dealing with oversight (now referenced, not repeated), the legal teeth of this proposal ensure neutrality is not merely advisory or aspirational—it becomes enforceable and irreversible except by the will of the people through referendum.

To guarantee transparency and long-term compliance, the Act proposes the creation of an independent constitutional body: the Irish Neutrality and Sovereignty Commission (INSC). This permanent commission would serve as the institutional guardian of Ireland's neutral status, providing legal scrutiny, public reporting, and proactive enforcement of the neutrality clause.

The Commission would be composed of twelve members, nominated by the Oireachtas and drawn from civil society, academia, retired judiciary, defence experts committed to non-alignment, and international representatives from other neutral states. Its structure would be balanced to avoid partisanship, ensuring its independence from government cycles and executive influence.

Key powers of the INSC would include:

- Reviewing all proposed treaties, international agreements, and EU defence-related measures for neutrality compliance;
- Publishing bi-annual Neutrality Compliance Reports detailing any actions or trends that risk infringing neutrality;
- Issuing binding injunctions if the government or military attempts to circumvent neutrality clauses through informal cooperation, back-channel diplomacy, or budgetary participation in non-neutral operations;
- Subpoena authority to access classified documents, interview ministers or defence officials, and launch inquiries into suspected breaches.

In addition to its watchdog role, the INSC would maintain a public education and engagement function, publishing simplified legal analyses of international agreements and explaining the implications of Irish involvement in emerging security arrangements.

One of the Commission's most vital functions would be activating a "constitutional review trigger"—a legal procedure whereby if three-quarters of the Commission believes the government has entered into a de facto military alignment, it can request a Supreme Court opinion on the constitutionality of such an arrangement. This trigger mechanism would ensure that neutrality is continuously protected, not only during treaty ratification but across the lifespan of Ireland's international obligations.

By embedding such a body in the Constitution and statute, the Act ensures neutrality is not an occasional principle, but a permanent feature of national governance—guarded by an institution that answers only to law and the people.

Central to the legitimacy of the Irish Neutrality and Sovereignty Act is the principle that neutrality must be owned by the people. To move neutrality from policy to constitutional principle requires a national referendum under Article 46 of Bunreacht na hÉireann. This referendum would propose a new article, to be inserted into the Constitution as Article 29B, outlining Ireland's permanent commitment to military neutrality.

The proposed constitutional text would read:

"Ireland affirms its permanent and positive neutrality.
The State shall not join or participate in any military alliance, including but not limited to mutual defence pacts or war coalitions. No foreign military base or combat infrastructure shall be located on Irish soil.

Ireland shall not permit its territory, airspace, or public assets to be used for military operations or preparations for war, unless expressly authorised by a mandate of the United Nations Security Council and approved by the Government and the Oireachtas.

This neutrality shall not prevent Ireland from participating in humanitarian missions, peacekeeping operations under the auspices of the United Nations, or in collective measures for the prevention or cessation of genocide, subject to parliamentary oversight and the principles of international law.

Any proposed amendment or repeal of this Article shall require approval by referendum."

This language balances clarity with flexibility. It defines the core principles of neutrality—non-participation in alliances, refusal to host foreign forces, and limitation of military cooperation—while still allowing Ireland to play a constructive role in international peace and humanitarian response.

The referendum would be accompanied by a statutory public information campaign, outlining the legal implications of the amendment, its relationship to existing treaty obligations (such as EU membership), and its operational limits (e.g. peacekeeping remains permitted). The campaign would also explain the oversight role of the INSC and the legal penalties for breach, already described in earlier segments.

If passed, the referendum would place Ireland among a select group of nations—like Austria and Switzerland—whose neutrality is not merely a diplomatic posture but a constitutional identity. It would remove the ambiguity that has plagued recent defence debates and grant legal and moral clarity to the Irish people in an age of growing global uncertainty.

In the decades since the foundation of the State, Ireland's foreign policy has been shaped by an enduring desire to remain independent—not just in name, but in action. Neutrality has been central to that aspiration. It has enabled Ireland to resist colonial legacies, avoid entanglement in great power rivalries, and build a reputation as a principled, peace-oriented democracy. But principles are only as strong as the structures that protect them.

This chapter has laid out a clear legal and constitutional framework to protect Ireland's neutrality from erosion, ambiguity, and manipulation. In doing so, it responds directly to the pressures outlined throughout this book: pressures from NATO, from EU defence integration, from economic coercion, and from shifting public narratives. Ireland's neutrality has been incrementally tested by informal military cooperation and European defence convergence. Economic stability and investor confidence hinge not only on tax policy but on the perception of Ireland as a neutral, non-aggressive, and globally respected nation.

Codifying neutrality through the Irish Neutrality and Sovereignty Act is, therefore, not merely an act of resistance—it is an act of renewal. It affirms that Ireland's strength lies not in war-making capacity, but in moral leadership, constitutional clarity, and democratic legitimacy. By holding a referendum and embedding neutrality into Bunreacht na hÉireann, the Irish people would reclaim sovereignty over a policy that has been increasingly shaped by quiet executive drift and external expectation.

Some will argue that constitutionalising neutrality restricts Ireland's flexibility. That it limits our capacity to "respond to threats." But this logic confuses independence with alignment. Ireland does not need to sacrifice its sovereignty to contribute to global peace. It can uphold international law, engage in peacekeeping, and offer humanitarian assistance—without joining military blocs or hosting foreign armies.

Others may argue that the world has changed—that neutrality is outdated. But that is exactly why it must now be protected. In a time when war, disinformation, and coercive diplomacy are resurging, neutrality is not a retreat—it is a strategic refusal to participate in permanent warfare. It is a vision of Ireland as a space of diplomacy, protection, and principle. And it is a model the world needs.

Constitutionalising neutrality would make Ireland the first country in modern Europe to place non-alignment at the heart of its national identity through direct public consent. It would send a message—to NATO, to the EU, to future Irish governments—that the people will decide the fate of their foreign policy, not foreign lobbies, backroom treaties, or bureaucratic drift.

Neutrality is not just a defence policy. It is a democratic claim. It is sovereignty, in the truest sense.

15

THE ENVIRONMENTAL COST OF MILITARIZATION

Militarization is often evaluated through the lens of security, strategy, and economics, but rarely through its environmental consequences. Yet the global military sector is one of the world's largest institutional polluters. From carbon emissions and toxic waste to soil degradation and ocean contamination, modern warfare and military preparedness leave a footprint that transcends battlefields and national borders.

Militaries consume vast quantities of fossil fuels. The U.S. Department of Defense alone emits more greenhouse gases annually than many medium-sized countries. Tanks, aircraft carriers, fighter jets, and long-range bombers require extraordinary fuel inputs, much of it derived from carbon-intensive sources. The construction, maintenance, and deployment of military infrastructure further exacerbate emissions—military bases are often energy-inefficient, sprawling across ecologically sensitive areas without proper environmental regulation.

Yet the environmental costs go far beyond emissions. Weapons testing, particularly of nuclear, biological, and chemical weapons, has left behind long-lasting contamination. The legacy of Cold War arsenals includes irradiated zones, poisoned aquifers, and abandoned test sites from the Nevada Desert to Kazakhstan. In many cases, military authorities have refused to disclose the full extent of environmental degradation, citing national security concerns. This opacity makes mitigation and public health responses slow, if not impossible.

Warzones themselves often become ecological dead zones. In Iraq and Afghanistan, the extensive use of heavy metals and depleted uranium munitions has not only devastated local populations but left ecosystems scarred for generations. Bombed oil refineries, scorched earth tactics, and mass deforestation—used both as a strategy of denial and terrain clearance—have permanently altered local climates and destroyed biodiversity.

The environmental impact also extends into the oceans. Naval operations, sonar testing, and live-fire exercises disrupt marine life, alter migration patterns, and contribute to oceanic noise pollution that is especially harmful to whales and other sonar-sensitive species. Chemical runoffs from coastal bases and shipyards further degrade marine habitats.

The cumulative effect of global militarization on the climate and biosphere is staggering, yet militaries are largely exempt from climate agreements. The 1997 Kyoto Protocol granted military emissions a carve-out, a precedent that continued into the Paris Agreement—where states were left to self-report or exclude defense sector emissions entirely. This legal loophole allows military pollution to grow unchecked, even as civilian sectors face increasing pressure to decarbonize.

Ireland, as a neutral nation, has a unique position. Its military emissions are among the lowest in the EU. This environmental dividend of neutrality is rarely acknowledged, but deeply significant. Unlike NATO states that must meet interoperability and readiness targets through intensive drilling, Ireland has avoided the large-scale war games, air patrols, and weapons stockpiling that generate carbon at industrial levels.

Militarization and climate change are no longer separate conversations. As the world faces environmental collapse, Ireland must consider not just the geopolitical implications of joining a military alliance, but the ecological cost of doing so. In an age where climate justice and peace are increasingly intertwined, neutrality is not merely a political position—it is a climate strategy.

In a world grappling with climate breakdown, the concept of sustainable defence is no longer a contradiction—it is a necessity. As militaries around the world begin to acknowledge their environmental impact, some states are exploring ways to reconcile security with sustainability. But in practice, the possibilities are limited. The very nature of large-scale militarization—its logistics, supply chains, training regimes, and weapons systems—is inherently resource-intensive. This is where Ireland's position as a neutral nation provides not only moral clarity but environmental foresight.

Neutrality enables Ireland to pursue a low-emission defence posture that is aligned with the Paris Climate Agreement and the Sustainable Development Goals. Without the operational burden of NATO obligations—such as mass-scale joint exercises, rapid response air deployments, and multinational naval operations—Ireland is free to develop a military capacity focused on peacekeeping, humanitarian response, and civil emergency preparedness. These missions require coordination and efficiency, but not the heavy environmental costs associated with offensive military readiness.

While NATO and EU defence policies increasingly mention climate change, the rhetoric has yet to produce transformation. For example, NATO's Climate and Security Agenda, unveiled in 2021, acknowledges climate risk to operational effectiveness but stops short of addressing the alliance's direct contribution to emissions. Similarly, the EU's defence initiatives—while incorporating elements of green procurement—remain committed to expanding the bloc's military-industrial capacity. Greenwashing remains a serious concern.

Ireland, by contrast, can lead by example. A neutral defence strategy allows for a holistic model in which environmental sustainability is not an afterthought but a guiding principle.

This includes:
- Developing **low-carbon military infrastructure**, powered by renewables and designed for dual civilian-defence use.
- Investing in **climate-resilient emergency response capabilities** that support both domestic crisis preparedness and UN peacekeeping missions.
- Prioritising **cybersecurity and intelligence-based deterrence** over carbon-heavy military projection.
- Redirecting defence spending toward **sustainable innovation**, such as autonomous rescue technologies and disaster monitoring satellites, that serve both civilian and peacekeeping ends.

This kind of sustainable defence policy does not mean disarmament—it means aligning military planning with planetary boundaries. Ireland's Defence Forces can and should be trained to respond to floods, wildfires, climate-induced displacement, and food insecurity. These are the emerging threats of the 21st century, and they demand an entirely different concept of national security—one in which the military protects not just sovereignty, but ecology.

Neutrality provides Ireland with the policy space and political freedom to innovate. Instead of expanding emissions-heavy training or importing foreign weapons systems with large carbon footprints, Ireland can direct its defence strategy toward resilience, adaptability, and international humanitarian leadership. It is a vision not just for military sustainability, but for a **post-militarised concept of security**, in which states protect ecosystems as part of national defence.

In doing so, Ireland could position itself at the forefront of a new global model—where neutrality enables environmental responsibility, and sustainable defence is not the exception, but the norm.

Among the most underreported forms of pollution is that generated by military activity. The scale of environmental degradation caused by armed forces—particularly those of major powers—is immense, spanning air, land, and sea. Unlike other sectors, military emissions are often excluded from national reporting, making the true ecological toll of war and war-readiness difficult to quantify. But the damage is real, and increasingly irreversible.

Carbon emissions are the most visible indicator of military pollution. Combat aircraft, tanks, and naval vessels consume vast quantities of fossil fuels. A single F-35 fighter jet, for example, burns over 5,600 litres of jet fuel per hour. A large aircraft carrier can consume hundreds of thousands of litres daily. Add to this the energy demands of operating sprawling bases, testing ranges, surveillance networks, and supply chains, and the emissions footprint of militaries becomes one of the world's largest institutional sources of greenhouse gases.

Yet these emissions are largely exempt from international climate agreements. Under the Kyoto Protocol and continued under the Paris Agreement, countries are not required to include military emissions in their national carbon inventories. This legal blind spot allows governments to trumpet progress on emissions reductions while their defence sectors remain unregulated and unaccountable.

Marine ecosystems are another casualty. Naval operations—including sonar testing, submarine patrols, and war game exercises—generate lethal underwater noise pollution. Sonar has been shown to interfere with marine mammal navigation, feeding, and migration patterns. Mass strandings of whales and dolphins have been linked to military sonar activity in the Atlantic and Pacific. These disturbances not only kill marine life directly but alter the acoustic habitat in ways that undermine entire food webs.

Explosive ordnance testing and the sinking of decommissioned ships for target practice also contribute to toxic leaching into seabeds. Corrosion from metal hulls, residue from propellants, and unexploded ordnance release harmful substances into marine environments for decades. In coastal areas near naval bases or weapons testing zones, these contaminants find their way into fisheries, disrupting biodiversity and threatening food safety.

The North Atlantic, where Ireland's territorial waters are located, is a zone of increasing military activity. NATO's naval drills and submarine patrols have expanded significantly since 2014 in response to geopolitical tensions with Russia. These operations risk turning Irish waters—known for their rich marine biodiversity and critical fisheries—into a de facto extension of the military-industrial complex.

Ireland's continued neutrality has so far shielded it from participating in these practices. But any alignment with NATO or a future EU defence force would likely change that. Participation in joint naval exercises, expanded surveillance, or anti-submarine operations would introduce new pollutants and disturbances into Ireland's Exclusive Economic Zone (EEZ). For a country whose economy and ecology are so intertwined with the sea, this would be more than a symbolic loss—it would be a practical and environmental catastrophe.

The environmental cost of militarization is not a distant problem. It is happening now—below the surface, beyond the headlines, and often beyond the reach of law. If Ireland remains neutral, it not only avoids complicity in these harms but preserves its ability to act as a responsible steward of the ocean, and a voice for demilitarised environmental policy.

Militarisation is not just a threat to peace—it is a threat to the planet. While much of the world debates emissions from cars, agriculture, and industry, the single largest unregulated contributor to climate and ecological collapse remains largely immune from scrutiny: the global military complex. And in this system, neutrality is not just a geopolitical stance—it is an environmental necessity.

As Ireland considers its future within an increasingly militarised EU and a world shaped by military alliances, it must ask a fundamental question: do we want to align ourselves with one of the most polluting sectors on Earth? NATO, for all its strategic cohesion, is a high-emissions entity. Its war games, troop deployments, and global reach leave trails of carbon, toxins, and disruption across continents and oceans. The EU's growing defence structures, including the European Defence Fund and PESCO, risk reproducing the same environmentally blind models under a new flag.

Ireland, by contrast, has a choice. As a neutral state, it already benefits from low military emissions. Its Defence Forces, while capable, are structured around civil protection, peacekeeping, and disaster response—not power projection. This is not a weakness—it is a blueprint. Neutrality offers Ireland the opportunity to design a sustainable model of national security that aligns with its climate commitments and ethical obligations.

Some argue that climate and defence must be treated separately. That national security comes first, and environmental concerns can be addressed later. But this argument collapses under scrutiny. What good is defending sovereignty if the soil is contaminated, the air is poisoned, and the seas are dead zones? What does national pride mean in a nation unlivable from the collateral damage of our own defence policies?

Others argue that NATO and the EU are adapting—that green procurement and "military sustainability" are on the rise. But these efforts are peripheral, voluntary, and often designed more for optics than outcomes. Carbon-neutral tanks and biodegradable bullets cannot solve the deeper contradiction of maintaining global peace through permanent readiness for war.

Ireland has a chance to lead by doing less. By refusing to join military alliances, it refuses to participate in their emissions. By enshrining neutrality in law, as proposed in Chapter 14, it protects both its sovereignty and its ecosystem. And by committing to sustainable defence, Ireland can pioneer a new model of planetary security—one based not on deterrence, but on diplomacy, disaster resilience, and environmental stewardship.

In a time of intersecting crises—climate, war, and democratic decline— neutrality is not passive. It is a position. It is a protest. It is a plan.

Ireland should not be drawn into military alliances that will leave its seas polluted, its skies militarised, and its economy redirected toward permanent preparedness. It should instead define its legacy as a green defender of peace—a nation that understood, before it was too late, that the cost of militarisation is more than just financial. It is existential.

16

IRELAND'S SURVIVAL IN A GLOBAL NUCLEAR WAR.

Including a chapter on nuclear war in a book about Irish neutrality may, to some, seem alarmist. But in 2025, the language of nuclear threats has moved from the shadows of Cold War hypotheticals into the foreground of daily political discourse. What was once the unthinkable is now routinely discussed by heads of state, military analysts, and NATO officials—from warnings to stockpile food and water, to renewed emphasis on "nuclear umbrellas." France has publicly reiterated its deterrent role. NATO's secretary general has made no secret of civil preparedness advice. And all the while, there is an eerie silence where diplomacy once stood. This is not scaremongering—it is realism. We now live in a world where posturing with apocalyptic consequences has become a staple of international relations. Ireland, despite its historic neutrality, is not immune. For those who prefer to put their heads in the sand, the warnings will come too late. This chapter exists not to provoke fear, but to confront the hard questions: How would Ireland survive in a nuclear conflict? What systems are in place—or missing entirely? And is neutrality, in this new age, a shield or a gamble?

In the event of a nuclear conflict—whether between NATO and Russia, China and the U.S., or multiple adversaries—Ireland's pre-war planning would determine not just survival rates, but the country's long-term ability to recover and retain sovereignty. Yet as of 2025, Ireland has no comprehensive national civil defence strategy tailored for nuclear war. This leaves the country uniquely exposed, despite rising global tensions and increased public awareness of nuclear risks.

Civil defence planning begins with public education, but there is currently no government-issued nuclear preparedness guide for citizens, no national awareness campaign on radiation risks, and no plan for mass evacuation or sheltering. This lack of basic information places citizens at immediate disadvantage should a crisis erupt. In contrast, Finland, Switzerland, and Austria—three historically neutral nations—have maintained active civil defence systems for decades, including underground shelters, national food reserves, and radiation contingency protocols. Ireland has none of these.

Food security is another critical component. In a global nuclear crisis, agricultural zones in major food-producing countries could be contaminated, leading to widespread shortages. Ireland's domestic agriculture, heavily export-oriented and dependent on imported fuel, fertilisers, and seed, would be ill-equipped to reorient quickly to serve national needs. While the country is a major dairy and meat exporter, its reliance on external supply chains for cereals, grains, and key nutrients presents a serious risk. Strategic stockpiling of shelf-stable foods does not currently exist in any meaningful form at the national level.

Energy resilience is equally fragile. Ireland's power grid relies heavily on imported fossil fuels and an increasingly interconnected European network. A continental blackout or interruption to undersea gas pipelines or interconnectors would plunge Ireland into darkness within hours. Unlike nations with independent energy storage and generation reserves, Ireland's electricity and heating systems lack both redundancy and national fallback capacity.

Government preparedness, therefore, must begin with three key pillars: (1) a civil defence communications plan, (2) national food sovereignty infrastructure, and (3) decentralised energy generation. Investment in community-level solar, microgrid systems, emergency water reserves, and secure local food storage networks could dramatically increase resilience. But such a programme would require both political will and public mobilisation—neither of which are currently evident.

The absence of these preparations is not merely an oversight—it is a failure of governance in the face of credible existential risk. The question for Ireland is no longer whether a nuclear war is likely, but whether the government can afford to leave its population unprepared for one of history's oldest and gravest threats.

If a nuclear exchange were to occur, Ireland's survival in the first 72 hours would hinge on basic measures that—at present—are almost entirely lacking. The absence of public fallout shelters, real-time radiation monitoring, and decentralised emergency response capabilities exposes a dangerous vulnerability in the country's disaster planning. While larger powers have developed shelter networks and civil defence coordination systems, Ireland has, in effect, made a silent bet that its neutral status will protect it. This assumption is increasingly outdated.

The most immediate threat following a nuclear detonation is radioactive fallout—especially in the event of a ground burst, which throws vast amounts of irradiated dust and debris into the atmosphere. Ireland, located downwind of numerous potential NATO and Russian targets in the UK and Europe, could face fallout within 6 to 24 hours, depending on prevailing winds. Without shelters, protective infrastructure, or public iodine distribution protocols, the population would be highly susceptible to acute radiation sickness, thyroid cancer, and long-term genetic damage.

Fallout shelters do not need to be sophisticated to save lives. Basic basement or underground structures, reinforced and stocked with water, non-perishable food, and ventilation filters, could drastically reduce exposure. Yet Ireland has no national shelter programme—no retrofitting of existing infrastructure, no municipal guidance on safe refuge zones, and no reserve of protective equipment for first responders. In contrast, Switzerland maintains shelter space for over 100% of its population. Ireland maintains virtually none.

Radiation monitoring is another critical gap. A robust post-strike response requires a distributed network of real-time geiger counters, satellite-linked observation stations, and mobile detection units. This allows authorities to map "hot zones," direct evacuations, and prevent secondary contamination from food or water sources. Ireland's current radiation detection capability is concentrated within the Environmental Protection Agency (EPA), but it is limited in scope and not integrated into a wartime response framework.

Emergency aid systems would also be overwhelmed. Ireland has no centralised authority tasked with nuclear triage, no stockpiles of burn treatments, potassium iodide tablets, or mobile decontamination units. Hospitals, already under strain from routine demands, lack the training and equipment to handle thousands of radiation-exposed patients.

In the short term, survival will depend on three actions: (1) immediate sheltering from fallout, (2) accurate identification of safe zones, and (3) access to emergency treatment and clean water. For this to be possible, the government must pre-position supplies, train emergency personnel, and educate the public on basic survival protocols.

Failure to prepare in this domain will not be an act of passive negligence—it will be a lethal omission. In the event of a nuclear incident, the first 72 hours will determine whether Ireland endures as a functioning society, or slips into chaos.

If Ireland were to survive the initial shock of a nuclear war—whether through luck, wind patterns, or the partial effectiveness of short-term emergency responses—it would still face an existential challenge: how to recover. Nuclear conflict is not a single-event crisis; it is a cascade of devastation whose impacts can last for years or even decades. For Ireland, long-term recovery would require a whole-of-society transformation across food systems, healthcare, infrastructure, and governance.

Ireland's agriculture sector—largely designed for export—would have to be radically restructured for self-sufficiency. Nuclear fallout contaminates soil, groundwater, and livestock. Crops grown in radioactive topsoil absorb isotopes such as cesium-137 and strontium-90, which then enter the human food chain. Rebuilding agriculture would therefore require both decontamination and a shift to controlled-environment agriculture, such as greenhouses and hydroponic systems.

Seed banks would need to be protected in secure underground vaults, and clean water access guaranteed via boreholes or distillation. Fertiliser inputs, often imported, would need to be manufactured domestically, and distribution networks decentralised. Farmers would also require training in radiation-safe practices and monitoring tools. The state would have to become the coordinator of a new agricultural sovereignty—less export-oriented and more resilient.

Ireland's healthcare system, already stretched in peacetime, would be devastated by nuclear conflict. Hospitals would face shortages of everything from antibiotics to clean linens, and long-term care for cancer, burns, respiratory conditions, and mental trauma would overwhelm existing capacity. Medical professionals may flee, fall ill, or be unable to report to work due to infrastructure collapse.

Long-term recovery would necessitate the rebuilding of regional hospitals with independent energy and water systems. Training new cohorts of medical professionals—especially in nuclear medicine and trauma psychiatry—would be essential. International medical cooperation, if still viable, would likely become a priority in diplomacy.

National recovery also hinges on restoring trust and functionality in institutions. Roads, rail, telecoms, and water systems may be partially or wholly destroyed. Digital infrastructure could remain compromised for years, requiring reversion to analogue backups. Cities may experience depopulation, and mass internal migration from contaminated areas to rural regions would strain housing and social services.

Governance would require emergency legal frameworks that balance civil liberties with survival measures. A Civil Reconstruction Authority (CRA) could be established to direct reconstruction, monitor radiation zones, and coordinate aid. Transparency would be vital; so too would preventing post-crisis authoritarianism under the guise of recovery.

In the long-term, Ireland would need to shift from dependence on global trade to domestic resilience. Neutrality, once seen as an ideal, would become essential to avoiding further involvement in external conflicts. The recovery from nuclear war is not just physical—it is moral, cultural, and political.

International law is not abandoned in the face of nuclear conflict—it becomes more critical than ever. Its frameworks, though often fragile under fire, represent the last institutional bulwarks against total annihilation. For Ireland, a neutral state under most definitions of international law, its legal posture in a nuclear war is shaped by a complex web of treaties, humanitarian obligations, and evolving norms of state behaviour.

First and foremost, Ireland is a signatory to the United Nations Charter, which enshrines the prohibition of the use of force in international relations, except in cases of self-defence or with the authorisation of the UN Security Council. This makes pre-emptive participation in war—particularly in nuclear-armed conflicts—legally problematic without a Security Council mandate. Even NATO's doctrine of "collective defence" under Article 5 operates outside the UN Charter's strict guidelines. Therefore, Ireland's potential involvement through alliance membership could place it at odds with its legal obligations under the Charter.

Ireland is also a party to the Treaty on the Non-Proliferation of Nuclear Weapons (NPT). As one of the earliest and most active supporters of global non-proliferation, Ireland's moral and legal reputation is tightly bound to its opposition to nuclear weapons. The NPT obligates non-nuclear states not to develop or host nuclear arms. If Ireland joined NATO and agreed to the deployment or transit of nuclear weapons through its ports or airspace, it could undermine its standing under this treaty—if not in legal fact, then certainly in global perception.

Additionally, Ireland has ratified the Treaty on the Prohibition of Nuclear Weapons (TPNW), which entered into force in 2021. While most nuclear-armed states and NATO members have not joined this treaty, Ireland's signature further codifies its commitment to nuclear disarmament. Under the TPNW, Ireland is prohibited from aiding or encouraging the use or threat of nuclear weapons—a provision that could be violated through indirect alliance entanglements, intelligence sharing, or logistical support to nuclear-capable operations.

The Hague and Geneva Conventions, as well as customary international humanitarian law, prohibit indiscriminate attacks, unnecessary suffering, and the targeting of civilians. Nuclear weapons, by their very nature, raise serious concerns under these laws. Any participation by Ireland—logistically or politically—in a conflict that involves nuclear targeting could place it at odds with the principle of distinction, the prohibition of superfluous injury, and the rule of proportionality.

Moreover, neutrality under The Hague Convention V (1907) carries specific rights and duties. A neutral state must not allow its territory to be used for military advantage by countries engaged in conflict. Hosting NATO logistics, allowing surveillance flights, or supporting war infrastructure could forfeit Ireland's neutral status, making it both legally and militarily vulnerable. If Ireland maintains a strict stance of neutrality. In that case, it can assert its right under international law to have its sovereignty respected by all parties involved in the conflict—a principle that, while frequently violated in modern warfare, still provides a vital foundation for diplomatic protest and international advocacy.

17

IRISH CASUALTY PROJECTIONS IN A NUCLEAR CONFLICT

Following the stark assessment of Ireland's vulnerabilities in a nuclear conflict, this chapter turns from infrastructure and preparedness to the most sobering measure of all: lives lost. This is not speculation for its own sake. It is realism—an attempt to allow the gravity of the situation to sink in. Where the previous chapter examined how Ireland might endure a nuclear crisis physically and institutionally, what follows forces us to reckon with its human toll. Discussing projected casualties in such a war is deeply uncomfortable, but necessary. It confronts us with the consequences of political choices too often debated in detached, abstract terms—like NATO membership or expanded EU military cooperation. These are not policy preferences without cost. They come with stakes that must be made visible and personal. The war drums no longer beat in the distance; they sound daily—through threats from Moscow, warnings from Washington, and a global slide into military posturing and diminished diplomacy. The scenarios explored here—whether a NATO-Russia clash, a U.S.–China confrontation, or a Middle East war—are not just strategic hypotheticals. They illuminate what war might mean for Irish families, neighborhoods, hospitals, and cities. These figures are not statistics on a spreadsheet. They are communities shattered, lives interrupted, futures erased. For a small, densely networked nation like Ireland, the idea that geography alone might shield us is no longer tenable. In this light, neutrality is not just a moral position or historical identity—it is a line of defence measured not in ideals, but in lives saved.

Projecting casualties in hypothetical conflicts is inherently uncertain—but also necessary. For a nation like Ireland, traditionally removed from direct war theatres yet increasingly pressured to align with military blocs, understanding the potential human cost of war is essential for informed public policy and constitutional decisions. This chapter presents an analytical framework for estimating Irish casualties under several plausible conflict scenarios, based on current military doctrine, strategic geography, and historical parallels.

Our methodology draws from three primary sources: (1) publicly available NATO and Russian military planning documents; (2) academic models on civilian and combatant casualties in urban and rural environments; and (3) World Health Organization (WHO) and UN data on radiation exposure, mass trauma care, and displacement trends. These projections are not speculative fiction—they reflect what could happen given existing capabilities, alliances, and strategic realities.

Key variables include:
- Ireland's military alignment (NATO member vs. neutral state);

- Conflict theatre (Europe, Pacific, Middle East);
- Target categories (military infrastructure, civilian population centers, or dual-use facilities like airports and ports);
- Weapon types (conventional, cyber, radiological, or nuclear);
- Collateral effects (infrastructure collapse, hospital overload, refugee influx, and supply chain breakdowns).

We also incorporate assumptions based on Ireland's current limitations:
- The country has no nuclear protection infrastructure (no missile defences, no fallout shelters);
- The Defence Forces lack rapid mobilisation capacity, with fewer than 10,000 full-time personnel;
- Emergency medical infrastructure is regionalised, with no reserve capacity for mass casualties;
- Most cities and towns are densely interlinked by fragile logistics, meaning an attack on one node—such as Shannon Airport or Dublin Port—could disrupt multiple systems.

Projections are broken into three tiers:
- Tier 1: Direct impact casualties (those killed in initial attacks or missile strikes);
- Tier 2: Indirect fatalities from infrastructure collapse, radiation, or starvation;
- Tier 3: Long-term casualties from disease, displacement trauma, and economic devastation.

Importantly, our estimates adjust for Ireland's geography. Its insular nature offers some natural protection, but its proximity to UK and EU NATO hubs also places it in harm's way if integrated militarily. Neutrality remains the single most significant variable in reducing projected casualties—but even in neutral scenarios, Ireland's interdependence with the global economy and European airspace makes it vulnerable to external shock.

This methodology is not intended to frighten, but to inform. These are not just numbers—they represent Irish families, communities, and futures. Understanding the cost of war is the first step toward defending peace.

War with Russia: Ireland as a NATO Staging Ground

In the event that Ireland joins NATO and a large-scale war breaks out between NATO and Russia, Ireland's role would rapidly shift from a peripheral actor to a strategic staging ground. While Ireland has no offensive nuclear capability and a limited defence budget, its geographic position between North America and Europe would make it vital for transatlantic logistics, surveillance, refuelling, and intelligence operations.

NATO's war planning, particularly since 2014, has placed heavy emphasis on reinforcing European positions from U.S. soil. Ireland's deep-sea ports, civilian airports like Shannon and Dublin, and civilian-military crossover infrastructure would be among the first to be militarised. This would transform civilian infrastructure into legitimate military targets.

Tier 1 (Direct Impact Casualties):
Assuming Ireland becomes a transatlantic link in NATO's war effort, Russian doctrine—which includes pre-emptive strikes on strategic infrastructure—would likely treat Irish ports and airfields as targets. An

attack on Shannon Airport or Dublin Port using conventional cruise missiles could cause an estimated 2,000–5,000 civilian deaths in surrounding areas, depending on time of day and strike accuracy. If dual-use buildings (such as logistics hubs, telecom towers, or data centres) are also struck, casualties could be even higher.

Tier 2 (Indirect Casualties):
Beyond the initial attacks, infrastructure disruption would lead to widespread power outages, fuel shortages, and food supply breakdowns. The National Grid, which relies heavily on digital command systems, would be highly vulnerable to cyberattack. If Ireland's urban centres lose electricity or communications for even 48 hours, hospitals would fail, cold chains would break, and civil order would deteriorate.

These disruptions could cause secondary mortality from exposure, dehydration, untreated chronic conditions, and fire. In a prolonged conflict, deaths from such indirect causes could range from 10,000 to 30,000 nationally, depending on the scope of attacks and the government's capacity to maintain basic services.

Tier 3 (Long-Term Casualties):
Should any attacks involve radiological or chemical components—whether in neighbouring NATO states or via transboundary fallout—Ireland would suffer long-term health effects. Increased cancer rates, birth defects, and mental health trauma could persist for decades. In such a scenario, Ireland might also become a destination for refugees fleeing the UK or mainland Europe, stretching resources and igniting political tension. A conservative estimate projects an additional 5,000–15,000 deaths over five years from

war-related secondary effects, including suicide, disease, and disrupted access to care.

Notably, all of these projections presume no nuclear detonation directly on Irish soil. If nuclear escalation occurs and Ireland is targeted—as explored in Chapter 16—casualty figures would rise exponentially into the hundreds of thousands.

This scenario demonstrates the grim reality: Ireland's NATO membership would not provide deterrence against Russian aggression—it would invite it. The cost, counted not in abstract threats but in Irish civilian lives, must be measured in advance, not in hindsight.

War with China: The U.S. and the Pacific Front

A war between the United States and China—likely centred on Taiwan or the South China Sea—would initially seem distant from Irish shores. But as with many global conflicts, the indirect consequences could be profound. If Ireland is a NATO member, or even deeply integrated through PESCO or other EU defence structures, its role in such a war would not be neutral. In that scenario, Ireland becomes both a participant in the global coalition and a secondary casualty of a war it did not start.

Ireland would not host troops or aircraft bound for the Pacific theatre, but its cyber infrastructure, data centres, and strategic position within the Western tech ecosystem would become central to NATO's digital warfare effort. Dublin hosts the European headquarters of many of the world's largest tech firms—Apple, Facebook (Meta), Google, Amazon Web Services, and Microsoft among them. These companies handle sensitive data and cloud infrastructure relied upon by U.S. and European defence, intelligence, and logistics operations.

Tier 1 (Direct Casualties – Cyber and Kinetic):
If China initiates or retaliates with cyberattacks on NATO countries, Ireland would likely be targeted for its digital infrastructure. Attacks on data centres, telecom providers, or undersea internet cables off the Irish coast could trigger blackouts, communication failures, and potential kinetic escalation. While a missile strike on Irish soil in this conflict is less probable than in a Russia–NATO scenario, it cannot be ruled out entirely if NATO expands the war theatre globally.

In such a case, an attack on a single major cloud facility or power hub near Dublin could cause hundreds of immediate civilian deaths and plunge a wide area into technological darkness, with cascading effects on hospitals, transport, and civil services.

Tier 2 (Indirect Casualties – Infrastructure and Services Collapse):
Ireland's economy and civil services depend on uninterrupted data flows. If digital infrastructure is degraded or destroyed, everything from emergency services to hospital systems could collapse. Telehealth appointments, bank payments, traffic control systems, and supply chain software would all be affected. Extended outages could lead to up to 5,000 indirect deaths in the first two weeks—especially among vulnerable populations reliant on medical devices, medication delivery, or heating.

Tier 3 (Long-Term and Economic Fallout):
Ireland's economy is tightly tethered to U.S. and Chinese trade. If the war escalates into a global economic freeze or sanctions spiral, Ireland could

lose access to key export markets, raw materials, and investment. Pharmaceutical supply chains, in particular, depend on inputs from Asia. Job losses, inflation, and social unrest would likely follow. Over the course of two years, this scenario could produce a further 10,000–20,000 premature deaths through health system collapse, suicide, and worsening poverty.

If Ireland remains neutral, the probability of direct targeting drops significantly. However, as a node in the Western digital economy, neutrality may offer limited protection from cyber or proxy attacks, particularly if U.S. operations are routed through infrastructure hosted in Ireland.

This underscores a chilling truth: the modern battlefield is no longer geographic—it is digital, economic, and infrastructural. And Ireland, by virtue of its tech economy, is already part of it.

War in the Middle East: Irish Casualties from Proxy Wars

While a major war in the Middle East may appear regionally confined, the reality is that Ireland—either as a neutral state or as a NATO/EU-aligned actor—would not be immune from its human consequences. With long-standing U.S. involvement in the region, EU defence entanglements, and Ireland's support infrastructure for peacekeeping and humanitarian operations, the risk of becoming implicated in proxy dynamics is real. In this scenario, casualties for Ireland are more likely to result from indirect consequences such as terrorism, reprisals, refugee flows, economic instability, and soft infrastructure vulnerabilities.

Tier 1 (Direct Casualties – Terrorism and Blowback):

If Ireland joins NATO or significantly deepens its EU defence commitments, it could be viewed by jihadist groups or Iranian proxies as part of the Western coalition involved in the conflict. While Ireland has historically avoided being a direct target of terrorism, increased participation in military alliances may shift its risk profile.

Embassies, consulates, tech offices, and NGOs with links to NATO-affiliated states could be targeted. An attack on a diplomatic compound, transport hub, or commercial centre could result in dozens to several hundred civilian deaths, depending on the scale of the incident. While not guaranteed, such risks increase proportionally with visible military alignment.

Tier 2 (Indirect Casualties – Refugees, Infrastructure Strain, and Civil Disruption):
A broader Middle Eastern conflict would likely trigger mass displacement. If neighbouring EU countries absorb millions of refugees, Ireland would be expected—especially as an EU member—to share the burden. This could strain housing, healthcare, education, and policing in urban centres already grappling with shortages.

Social friction might increase as services are overwhelmed. Hospitals could experience patient overflow, leading to delayed treatment and increased non-conflict mortality—especially among the elderly and chronically ill. Over 12 to 24 months, Ireland could experience 1,000–3,000 additional deaths from indirect service failures or stress-related conditions if no adequate emergency planning is in place.

Tier 3 (Economic and Humanitarian Fallout):
A Middle East war would almost certainly disrupt global oil supply lines, increasing fuel prices and triggering inflation. Irish households and small

businesses, already sensitive to energy shocks, would suffer. If fuel scarcity forces rationing, transportation of food and medical goods could become erratic. Economic contraction would follow, potentially pushing thousands below the poverty line.

Ireland also deploys humanitarian personnel through the Defence Forces and Irish Aid to conflict and post-conflict zones. If operations escalate or aid convoys are targeted, Irish peacekeepers or aid workers could be injured or killed in the field. Historically low, such risks may increase depending on the hostility of the environment and the scale of Ireland's engagement.

In summary, war in the Middle East poses a lower immediate kinetic threat to Ireland compared to NATO-Russia or U.S.-China war scenarios. However, the cumulative toll through refugee crises, terrorism, and economic shock would be significant. As a NATO or EU military participant, Ireland would no longer be seen as a neutral humanitarian actor but as a soft target in a polarised conflict landscape.

The analysis presented in this chapter leads to a singular conclusion: war, whether near or distant, would extract a heavy and multi-layered toll on Ireland. While historically regarded as a neutral state on the periphery of Europe, Ireland's global integration—through trade, digital infrastructure, diplomatic obligations, and defence debates—now places it within reach of modern war's human consequences.

Across the three examined scenarios—conflict with Russia, China, and within the Middle East—the projected casualties range from hundreds in targeted terrorist attacks to tens of thousands through systemic collapse, secondary effects, and displaced population stress. Each scenario shares a common denominator: the blurring of combatant and civilian. Whether it be a cyber strike on a hospital server, a missile launched at a NATO-refuelling hub, or a refugee crisis overloading a small coastal community, war in the 21st century leaves no state untouched, regardless of size or posture.

The difference lies in neutrality versus alignment. In every case modelled, Ireland's casualty projections are lower—sometimes dramatically so—if the state remains neutral and refrains from military alignment with NATO or an EU defence pact. The data suggests that while neutrality does not render Ireland immune to conflict spillover, it significantly reduces the likelihood of direct targeting and expands the space for diplomatic protection and public legitimacy.

Moreover, alignment would transform Ireland's infrastructure into military assets—Shannon Airport, Cork Port, even data centres in Dublin—and therefore legitimate targets in the eyes of adversaries. Neutrality offers no absolute guarantees, but it does maintain legal, strategic, and moral boundaries that many warring states have historically respected, at least in part.

A further layer of analysis reveals that the long-term casualties from economic collapse, mental trauma, and post-war health degradation may ultimately exceed the death toll from kinetic attacks. This is particularly true for a small island nation with limited emergency stockpiles, no missile defence capability, and heavy dependence on global supply chains for energy, medicine, and food.

Ireland's civil infrastructure is not built for war. Its hospitals lack mass casualty readiness. Its emergency services are understaffed and under-equipped for radiological or cyber-disaster scenarios. Even modest urban attacks could cripple Dublin, Cork, or Galway. Protracted energy shortages could cause hundreds to perish in rural areas. And if economic collapse follows, the austerity that comes after conflict could be deadlier than the war itself.

The human cost of war for Ireland would be measured not only in bombs or bullets—but in breadlines, blackouts, and broken systems. Each decision Ireland makes—on NATO, EU defence, or neutrality—must be made with this truth in mind.

Protecting lives means understanding the stakes. And if neutrality continues to offer the most protection to Irish civilians in times of global upheaval, it is not simply a principle. It is a policy of survival.

18

ABOUT THE AUTHOR

Ty Murphy, LLB, LLM, is a specialist in fine art due diligence, law, and investigations, including AML, KYC, CTF, and Sanctions. His multifaceted career spans high-value art transactions, legal advisory, media, and the creative industries. Originally from Cork City, Ireland, he has built an international reputation as a trusted advisor to collectors, investors, and institutions navigating the complexities of the global art market.

Ty's academic background reflects his diverse expertise. He studied art and life drawing at the Royal Academy of England, holds both an LLB and LLM in law from BPP University, and furthered his education in multiple disciplines, including writing and editing at Caerleon University in South Wales, psychotherapy and relationship therapy at Lancashire University, and directing at Bournemouth University. This breadth of knowledge has enriched his work across law, media, and the arts, allowing him to approach complex topics with both analytical precision and creative insight.

His expertise in the art market is widely sought after, particularly among Family Offices and UHNWI (Ultra-High-Net-Worth Individuals). He currently serves as Head of Acquisitions for the Es Revellar Art Resort and Museums, curating and overseeing one of Europe's most prestigious private art collections.

Beyond his advisory work, Ty is a leading voice in the art, finance, and publishing sectors, frequently delivering keynote speeches at global conferences, family office events, and investor summits. His expertise covers due diligence in fine art transactions, investing in blue-chip art, and legal complexities in the art world.

He is also a respected writer, editor, and publisher, serving as Editor and Publisher of *Art & Museum Magazine* and *Family Office Magazine*, two leading publications in their respective fields. His written works include *The Art Market: A Guide for Professionals and Collectors* and *The Art Market: Training Household Staff to Care for Art & Antiques*, and he is currently completing *The Art Law, Tax, and Business Handbook*. Additionally, his insights regularly appear in global media outlets such as CNN, Forbes and CNBC, where he provides expert commentary on art market trends, legal and tax regulations, and emerging challenges in the global art trade.

A creative at heart, Ty has extensive experience in the creative industries, blending his legal and business acumen with his artistic and media background. He is currently the host of the upcoming TV show *The Art Guy*, which will take viewers inside the world of high-end blue-chip art collecting and investment. His work in television, writing, and directing showcases his passion for storytelling and education.

Ty is also actively engaged in museum and scholarly initiatives, serving on the committees of the five Springfield Museums, acting as an advisor to the

Online Picasso Project, which is developing the new Picasso Catalogue Raisonné, and consulting for the Modigliani Institute.

With his deep knowledge of law, finance, global policy, and the creative industries, Ty Murphy now turns his attention to Ireland's neutrality debate in *Triple Lock & Neutrality: Ireland at a Crossroads*. This book provides an accessible yet thorough analysis of the forces shaping Ireland's role in global security, offering readers critical insights into one of the country's most pressing political and legal issues.

Appendix A

Constitutional Provisions Relevant to Irish Neutrality and the Triple Lock

Article 29 – International Relations

29.1
Ireland affirms its devotion to the ideal of peace and friendly co-operation amongst nations founded on international justice and morality.

29.2
Ireland affirms its adherence to the principle of the pacific settlement of international disputes by international arbitration or judicial determination.

29.3
Ireland accepts the generally recognised principles of international law as its rule of conduct in its relations with other States.

29.4.1°
The executive power of the State in or in connection with its external relations shall, in accordance with Article 28 of this Constitution, be exercised by or on the authority of the Government.

29.4.9°
The State shall not adopt a decision taken by the European Council to

establish a common defence pursuant to Article 42 of the Treaty on European Union where that common defence would include the State.

Article 28 – The Government

28.3.3°
Nothing in this Constitution other than Article 15.5.2° shall be invoked to invalidate any law enacted by the Oireachtas which is expressed to be for the purpose of securing the public safety and the preservation of the State in time of war or armed rebellion.

These articles form the **constitutional backbone** of Ireland's traditional stance on neutrality, its role in international law, and the constraints placed on government participation in military alliances or wartime actions. They are central to understanding how the **Triple Lock mechanism** functions both as policy and in light of constitutional obligations.

Appendix B

Timeline of Key Events in Irish Neutrality

Pre-World War II

- 1922 – Irish Free State established; remains neutral during internal conflicts but lacks a formal neutrality policy.
- 1932 – Éamon de Valera becomes Taoiseach (Prime Minister), emphasizing sovereignty and distancing from British military influence.

World War II (1939–1945) – "The Emergency"

- 1939 – Ireland declares neutrality at the outbreak of WWII, refusing to join the Allies or Axis powers.
- 1941 – Dublin bombed by Germany (accidental, but highlights neutrality risks).
- 1945 – Ireland maintains neutrality despite Allied pressure; refuses to expel German and Japanese diplomats.

Cold War Era (1945–1991)

- 1949 – Ireland refuses to join NATO, citing neutrality and partition (Northern Ireland remains under UK control).

- 1955 – Joins the United Nations (UN) but maintains neutrality in military alliances.
- 1961–1964 – Irish troops participate in UN peacekeeping missions (Congo), reinforcing neutrality with humanitarian engagement.
- 1973 – Joins the European Economic Community (EEC, later EU) but avoids military commitments.

Post-Cold War (1991–Present)

- 1999 – Ireland joins NATO's Partnership for Peace (PfP) but remains outside full NATO membership.
- 2003 – Refuses to support the US-led Iraq War, denying use of Shannon Airport for military purposes (though allows refueling).
- 2008 – Lisbon Treaty ratified with guarantees protecting Irish neutrality.
- 2022 – Russian invasion of Ukraine sparks debate on neutrality; Ireland supports EU sanctions but rules out NATO membership.
- 2023 – Establishes a Consultative Forum on International Security Policy, reviewing neutrality in light of global conflicts

Appendix C

List of Relevant Treaties and Agreements

- The Hague Convention V (1907)
  Outlines the rights and responsibilities of neutral powers in times of war. It serves as a legal foundation for Ireland's conduct and obligations as a neutral state.

- UN Charter (1945)
  Especially Articles 2(4) and 51: These govern the use of force and self-defense under international law, framing much of Ireland's approach to neutrality and peacekeeping.

- NATO (North Atlantic Treaty, 1949)
  While Ireland is not a member, the treaty's mutual defense clause (Article 5) and NATO's expanding operations have direct implications for Irish neutrality.

- Geneva Conventions and Additional Protocols (1949, 1977)
  Set out the rules of war and protection for civilians. These conventions guide Ireland's humanitarian and legal obligations in armed conflict scenarios.

- UN Peacekeeping Operations Agreements
  Ireland's involvement in peacekeeping missions is authorized through these, typically under UN Security Council mandates, aligning with the Triple Lock framework.

- European Economic Community Treaty (1957)
  Ireland joined the EEC in 1973. Although initially economic, it laid the groundwork for further political and defense cooperation within the EU.

- Treaty of the European Union (Maastricht Treaty, 1992)
  Established the EU's Common Foreign and Security Policy (CFSP), which includes optional defense cooperation frameworks Ireland has had to navigate carefully.

- NATO Partnership for Peace (PfP, 1994)
  Ireland joined in 1999, signaling limited cooperation with NATO without committing to mutual defense obligations.

- Treaty of Nice (2001) and Lisbon Treaty (2007)
  Introduced provisions for deeper EU defense integration. Irish ratification was contingent on protocols protecting neutrality, including guarantees that Ireland would not be obliged to join a common defense without a referendum.

- PESCO – Permanent Structured Cooperation (2017)
  An EU initiative for closer defense cooperation. While voluntary, Ireland's participation has raised concerns about neutrality dilution.

- Rome Statute of the International Criminal Court (1998)
  Establishes legal standards for war crimes and crimes against humanity. Ireland is a signatory, emphasizing its commitment to lawful international conduct.

- United Nations Convention on the Law of the Sea (UNCLOS, 1982)
  Relevant for Ireland's maritime surveillance and Exclusive Economic Zone (EEZ), particularly in neutrality enforcement and undersea cable defense.

- NIS2 Directive (EU, 2023)
  A cybersecurity regulation mandating digital defense measures that, while civilian in nature, may intersect with military and sovereignty concerns.

- Convention on Cluster Munitions (2008)
  Ireland is a signatory, prohibiting use, transfer, and stockpiling of cluster munitions—a symbolic stance reinforcing its humanitarian commitments.

- Cybercrime Act 2017 (Ireland)
  National legislation targeting cyber threats. Relevant in the discussion on extending neutrality into the cyber domain.

Appendix D

Directory of Organizations and Activists

Irish-Based Organizations

- Irish Neutrality League
  A grassroots group campaigning for the preservation of Ireland's traditional non-aligned stance and opposing Irish involvement in EU or NATO military projects.
  Website: www.irishneutralityleague.org

- PANA – Peace and Neutrality Alliance
  Founded in 1996, PANA advocates for Irish neutrality, withdrawal from NATO-related programs, and greater democratic control over foreign policy.
  Website: www.pana.ie

- Shannonwatch
  A watchdog group documenting and protesting the use of Shannon Airport by foreign military forces, especially the U.S. military.
  Website: www.shannonwatch.org

- Afri – Action from Ireland

An Irish NGO that promotes peace, justice, and sustainability, with long-standing opposition to militarization and support for neutrality.
Website: www.afri.ie

- Irish Anti-War Movement (IAWM)
  A network of activists and academics opposing Ireland's complicity in foreign wars and advocating non-interventionist policies.
  Website: www.irishantiwar.org

- Neutrality Matters (Campaign Platform)
  A public advocacy campaign calling for a referendum to protect Irish neutrality in the Constitution.
  Website: www.neutralitymatters.ie

International Organizations

- United Nations Department of Peace Operations (DPO)
  Coordinates global peacekeeping missions. Ireland has a long history of participation under UN mandates consistent with neutrality.
  Website: peacekeeping.un.org

- European Network Against Arms Trade (ENAAT)
  Tracks EU militarization and arms industry lobbying, including Ireland's involvement in PESCO and EU defense funds.
  Website: www.enaat.org

- War Resisters' International (WRI)
  A global pacifist network opposing war and militarism, advocating for conscientious objection and neutrality worldwide.
  Website: www.wri-irg.org

- Campaign for Nuclear Disarmament (CND – UK and International)
  Though UK-based, CND's outreach includes Ireland. They work against NATO expansion and nuclear weapon proliferation.
  Website: www.cnduk.org

Key Public Figures & Advocates

- Roger Cole
  Founder of PANA, a prominent voice in Irish anti-militarization and pro-neutrality advocacy.
  Noted for: Leading national debates, speaking at Oireachtas committees, and organizing public awareness campaigns.

- Dr. Karen Devine
  Political scientist and academic expert on Irish neutrality. Known for her published research and media commentary.
  Affiliation: Dublin City University (DCU)

- Clare Daly MEP
  Former Irish Member of the European Parliament outspoken on military neutrality, NATO criticism, and human rights.
  Social: @ClareDalyMEP

- Mick Wallace MEP
  Former Independent MEP aligned with Daly, known for his opposition to EU militarization and support for Irish neutrality.
  Social: @wallacemick

- John Lannon
  Coordinator of Shannonwatch and consistent campaigner against military use of civilian infrastructure.
  Noted for: Advocacy at the UN and EU levels on neutrality breaches.

Appendix E

Summary: The North Atlantic Treaty (1949)

(Also known as the Washington Treaty)

The North Atlantic Treaty, signed in Washington, D.C., on April 4, 1949, established the North Atlantic Treaty Organization (NATO). It is the alliance's foundational legal document, binding its members to mutual defense and cooperation in political, military, and security matters. Although Ireland is not a NATO member, the treaty has significant implications for Irish neutrality due to the geopolitical role NATO plays in Europe and the pressures it exerts on non-member states.

Preamble

The treaty begins by affirming the desire of member states to:

"live in peace with all peoples and all governments" and to "unite their efforts for collective defence and for the preservation of peace and security."

Key Articles Relevant to Irish Neutrality

Article 1 – Peaceful Resolution of Disputes
Members commit to:

"settle any international dispute in which they may be involved by peaceful means… and to refrain from the threat or use of force."

This language mirrors principles found in Article 29 of the Irish Constitution, underscoring a shared rhetorical commitment to peace. However, NATO's record of military interventions without UN mandates raises concerns about divergence in practice.

Article 5 – Collective Defence (Mutual Assistance Clause)

"An armed attack against one or more of them… shall be considered an attack against them all…"

This is the cornerstone of NATO's function: an attack on any member state is considered an attack on all, triggering military response obligations. If Ireland joined NATO, this clause would effectively override its neutral status, obligating it to participate in military operations potentially without UN approval.

Article 6 – Scope of Article 5
Defines what qualifies as an "armed attack," including attacks on member territories in Europe or North America, as well as forces, vessels, or aircraft operating in these regions.

Article 10 – Open Door Policy

"The Parties may, by unanimous agreement, invite any other European State… to accede to this Treaty."

This clause allows for NATO enlargement. Ireland has never applied for membership but is under periodic pressure to align more closely through programs like Partnership for Peace (PfP) and increased EU-NATO interoperability.

Article 13 – Withdrawal
Any party may withdraw from the Treaty one year after giving notice to the United States Government.

Relevance to Ireland

Though not a signatory, Ireland's foreign and defense policy is deeply affected by NATO's activities and strategic posturing:

- Shannon Airport has been used by NATO members (particularly the U.S.) for military logistics, raising legal and political questions.
- EU-NATO cooperation—particularly through PESCO and joint defence procurement—has brought Ireland into closer alignment with NATO goals, despite constitutional commitments to neutrality.
- Any future Irish membership in NATO would require a referendum, as per legal guarantees secured in EU treaty opt-outs and Article 29.4.9° of the Constitution.

The North Atlantic Treaty embodies a mutual defense pact incompatible with Ireland's long-standing policy of military neutrality. While Ireland cooperates with NATO on peacekeeping and cybersecurity through PfP, full membership would require a constitutional overhaul and a fundamental shift in Ireland's international identity. Understanding the legal structure and obligations of this treaty is essential to grasping the geopolitical forces shaping the neutrality debate today.

Appendix F

United Nations Charter – Key Articles Relevant to Neutrality

The Charter of the United Nations, signed on 26 June 1945 and in force since 24 October 1945, serves as the founding document of the UN and the legal bedrock of international peace and security. Ireland, as a committed member of the UN, grounds its foreign policy and neutrality in the Charter's core principles.

The Triple Lock mechanism—requiring United Nations Security Council authorization before Irish troops are deployed abroad—is directly linked to the legitimacy and framework of the UN Charter. The following articles are especially relevant:

Article 2(4) – Prohibition of the Use of Force

"All Members shall refrain in their international relations from the threat or use of force against the territorial integrity or political independence of any state, or in any other manner inconsistent with the Purposes of the United Nations."

This is a cornerstone principle of international law and underpins Ireland's constitutional commitment to peace (Article 29.1). It forbids aggression and militarism, making any foreign military intervention illegitimate without UN authorization—hence the importance of Article 2(4) in defending Ireland's neutrality.

Article 5 – Suspension of Rights of Aggressor States

"A Member of the United Nations against which preventive or enforcement action has been taken by the Security Council may be suspended from the exercise of the rights and privileges of membership by the General Assembly upon the recommendation of the Security Council."

This article provides a mechanism for limiting the influence of aggressor states within the UN. It further legitimizes Ireland's reliance on Security Council decisions in the deployment of troops and affirms the international legal order as a condition for engagement, reinforcing the structure of the Triple Lock.

Article 51 – Right to Self-Defence

"Nothing in the present Charter shall impair the inherent right of individual or collective self-defence if an armed attack occurs against a Member of the United Nations… until the Security Council has taken measures necessary to maintain international peace and security."

This article affirms the natural right of states to defend themselves in the face of attack, pending Security Council intervention. For Ireland, which has no standing army of significant scale and a policy of military non-alignment, this provision underscores the importance of international law and UN authorization as a shield in lieu of military alliances.

Relevance to Ireland

- Ireland's use of the Triple Lock aligns with Article 2(4) and Article 51, ensuring any foreign military deployment is lawful and peace-oriented.
- The Charter reaffirms the UN as Ireland's primary multilateral engagement in foreign affairs—an institution through which peacekeeping, not war-making, defines Irish identity.

- These articles also serve as a legal benchmark against which military alliances like NATO and defense integration projects like PESCO must be measured.

The UN Charter, especially Articles 2(4), 5, and 51, embodies the legal and ethical framework that Ireland has consistently relied upon to shape its foreign policy and protect its sovereignty. These provisions are foundational to Ireland's claim to neutrality and provide the international legitimacy underpinning the Triple Lock mechanism. Any attempt to bypass the UN's authority in matters of war and peace undermines the very principles upon which Ireland's neutrality has been constructed.

Appendix G

UN Security Council Resolution 1244 (1999) – Mandate for KFOR in Kosovo

UNSC Resolution 1244, adopted on 10 June 1999, authorized the deployment of international security and civil presence in Kosovo after the NATO bombing campaign against the Federal Republic of Yugoslavia. It serves as a foundational document for the NATO-led Kosovo Force (KFOR) and illustrates the critical role of the UN Security Council in legitimizing military deployments under international law.

This resolution is especially relevant to Ireland's foreign policy because it represents a case where Ireland contributed troops under the Triple Lock mechanism—with full UN, Government, and Dáil approval.

Legal and Political Significance

Authorizes international military presence (KFOR):

Paragraph 7 of the resolution explicitly authorizes NATO and other forces "to establish a secure environment" in Kosovo, confirming the Security Council's primacy in granting legitimacy to peace enforcement operations.

Reaffirms UN primacy:

Resolution 1244 reaffirms the UN's "leading role in the international civil and security presence," distinguishing this mission from unilateral or unauthorized military interventions. For Ireland, this distinction is crucial in preserving the legal integrity of neutrality.

Foundation for Triple Lock Deployment:

Ireland's participation in KFOR stands as a clear example of how the Triple Lock enables the country to participate in international peacekeeping without compromising neutrality. The mission was viewed as lawful, humanitarian, and UN-mandated.

Key Provisions from Resolution 1244

Paragraph 5:

"Authorizes the Secretary-General, with the assistance of relevant international organizations, to establish an international civil presence in Kosovo..."

Paragraph 7:

"Authorizes member states and relevant international organizations to establish an international security presence with substantial NATO participation to ensure the withdrawal of Yugoslav forces..."

Paragraph 9:

Tasks the international presence with ensuring public safety and order, demilitarization of armed groups, and support for humanitarian and reconstruction efforts.

Ireland's Role in KFOR

Ireland deployed troops to Kosovo under the auspices of this resolution. The deployment was lawful, supported by:

1. UN Security Council authorization (Resolution 1244),
2. Irish Government approval, and
3. Dáil Éireann consent.

This operation stands as a textbook example of how Irish neutrality, when framed by international law and democratic approval, is compatible with peacekeeping and humanitarian engagement abroad.

UNSC Resolution 1244 (1999) represents a landmark moment in post-Cold War international relations. It illustrates how the UN Security Council serves as the legal gateway for peacekeeping missions, and how Ireland can—and does—contribute to such missions without undermining its constitutional and moral commitment to neutrality.

By reinforcing the centrality of the UN mandate, Resolution 1244 strengthens the case for retaining and defending the Triple Lock, and for ensuring that any future Irish military engagement abroad continues to meet the highest standards of international legitimacy and democratic oversight.

Appendix H

UN Security Council Resolution 1973 (2011) – Legal Basis for NATO's Libya Operation

UNSC Resolution 1973, adopted on 17 March 2011, authorized member states to take "all necessary measures" to protect civilians under threat in Libya during the uprising against Muammar Gaddafi's regime. While presented as a humanitarian intervention, its aftermath raised serious legal and ethical questions—especially regarding the scope of force, civilian casualties, and regime change operations. For Ireland, this resolution is a cautionary case study on the risks of relying solely on UN authorization without clearly defined limits or oversight.

Overview and Legal Framework

Resolution 1973 was passed under Chapter VII of the UN Charter, which permits enforcement action in response to threats to peace, breaches of peace, or acts of aggression. The resolution:

- Imposed a no-fly zone over Libyan airspace;
- Authorized "all necessary measures" to protect civilians and civilian-populated areas;

- Strengthened the arms embargo and asset freezes from earlier resolutions;

Explicitly excluded a foreign occupation force on any part of Libyan territory.

Key Excerpts from Resolution 1973

Paragraph 4:

"Authorizes Member States... to take all necessary measures... to protect civilians and civilian populated areas under threat of attack in the Libyan Arab Jamahiriya..."

Paragraph 6:

"Decides to establish a ban on all flights in the airspace of the Libyan Arab Jamahiriya in order to help protect civilians..."

Paragraph 9:

"Calls upon all Member States... to ensure strict implementation of the arms embargo..."

Paragraph 13:

"Decides that Member States shall deny permission to any aircraft registered in Libya or owned by Libyan nationals to take off, land or overfly their territory unless for humanitarian purposes..."

NATO's Operation Unified Protector

Under this resolution, NATO launched Operation Unified Protector, which included:

- Aerial bombardments;
- Targeting of Libyan military infrastructure;

- Support for rebel forces;
- Ultimately, enabling the collapse of the Gaddafi regime.

Critics argued that the operation far exceeded the civilian protection mandate, effectively functioning as a regime change intervention without a subsequent UN resolution.

Implications for Ireland and Neutrality

While Ireland did not participate militarily, the broad interpretation of Resolution 1973 by NATO raised red flags for countries like Ireland that rely on UN mandates as a legal safeguard for military operations under the Triple Lock.

The Libya intervention illustrates how even UN-authorized operations can drift from humanitarian objectives to full-scale military campaigns, calling into question the reliability of "all necessary measures" as a legal standard.

For Irish policymakers and neutrality advocates, the Libya case underscores the importance of maintaining not just UN authorization, but clear national democratic control—as enshrined in the Triple Lock.

UNSC Resolution 1973 (2011) is a pivotal example of how well-intentioned multilateral mandates can be co-opted into broader military objectives, blurring the line between peacekeeping and war-making. For Ireland, which grounds its neutrality in strict international legality and moral restraint, the Libya precedent justifies a cautious and critically engaged approach to any future military authorization—UN-backed or not.

This case reinforces the need for transparency, proportionality, and parliamentary oversight in the deployment of Irish troops and the preservation of Ireland's constitutional commitment to peace.

Appendix I

European Court of Human Rights Rulings – Cases Against Poland and Others for CIA Black Site Cooperation

Following the September 11 attacks, the United States launched a covert program of "extraordinary rendition" in which individuals suspected of terrorism were abducted, transferred across borders without legal process, and subjected to secret detention and torture. Investigations revealed that several European countries had cooperated with this program by hosting or enabling CIA-operated black sites—in violation of both international human rights law and their own constitutional obligations.

These cases hold particular relevance for Ireland, which faces legal and ethical scrutiny over the use of Shannon Airport by the U.S. military, including suspected involvement in rendition flights. The rulings below offer precedents in accountability and state responsibility for complicity in unlawful foreign operations on national territory.

Key ECHR Cases

1.

Al Nashiri v. Poland (Application no. 28761/11, Judgment of 24 July 2014)

- Facts: Abd al-Rahim al-Nashiri, a Saudi national, was detained by the CIA and subjected to torture at a black site in Poland before being transferred to Guantanamo Bay.

Findings: The Court ruled that Poland:

- Allowed its territory to be used for CIA torture and incommunicado detention;
- Violated Articles 3 (prohibition of torture), 5 (right to liberty), 6 (right to a fair trial), 8 (right to private life), and Protocol 1, Article 1 (protection of property);
- Failed to conduct an effective investigation into the allegations.

2.

Abu Zubaydah v. Poland (Application no. 7511/13, Judgment of 24 July 2014)

- Facts: Zubaydah, a stateless Palestinian, was detained and tortured at the same CIA site in Poland.
- Findings: Mirroring Al Nashiri, the Court found Poland in clear breach of the European Convention on Human Rights, holding that it knowingly facilitated CIA abuses and failed to protect human dignity and national sovereignty.

3.

El-Masri v. North Macedonia (Application no. 39630/09, Judgment of 13 December 2012)

- Facts: Khaled El-Masri, a German citizen, was abducted in error by the CIA in Macedonia, rendered to Afghanistan, and tortured.

Findings: The ECHR held that Macedonia:

- Was responsible for unlawful detention, ill-treatment, and extraordinary rendition;
- Violated Articles 3, 5, 8, and 13 of the European Convention;
- Was complicit in CIA-led violations of international law.

Legal and Policy Implications

These rulings confirm that European states are legally accountable for human rights abuses committed by foreign powers when those abuses are facilitated or tolerated on national soil.

The Court emphasized that state sovereignty and human dignity cannot be overridden by alliance loyalty or informal agreements with powerful military partners.

These cases demonstrate that even passive complicity, such as granting access to airports, airspace, or intelligence services, can lead to international liability.

Relevance to Ireland

While no ECHR case has (yet) been brought against Ireland, substantial evidence and testimonies link Shannon Airport to CIA rendition flights, particularly during the Iraq and Afghanistan wars.

These precedents suggest that failure to investigate or prevent the use of Irish territory for unlawful foreign military or intelligence operations may constitute a violation of the European Convention on Human Rights.

They underscore the fragility of neutrality in the absence of robust oversight, and reinforce the need for transparency, accountability, and legal safeguards—as proposed in this book's recommendation for a Neutrality and Sovereignty Act.

The ECHR rulings against Poland, Macedonia, and others highlight the real-world consequences of abandoning vigilance in the name of cooperation or convenience. For Ireland, these cases are not distant legal oddities—they are warnings. If Ireland allows foreign powers to operate unchecked on its territory, it risks not only its moral standing and neutrality—but its compliance with international human rights law.

Appendix J:

Proposed Legal Frameworks and Oversight Mechanisms to Protect Irish Neutrality

1. The Irish Neutrality and Sovereignty Act (Proposed Constitutional Amendment)

A cornerstone of this book's legal strategy, the proposed Act would enshrine neutrality in the Irish Constitution as a permanent and positive principle. It would prohibit:

- Participation in military alliances;
- Hosting of foreign military bases or combat infrastructure;
- Use of Irish territory, airspace, or public infrastructure for foreign military operations.

Exceptions would apply only to:

- UN-mandated peacekeeping operations;
- Humanitarian interventions authorized by the **Triple Lock** mechanism.

Sample constitutional text (Article 29B) is proposed in the book:

"Ireland affirms its permanent and positive neutrality... Any proposed amendment or repeal of this Article shall require approval by referendum."

2. Criminal Enforcement Measures

To give legal teeth to neutrality, the Act proposes to **criminalize**:

- Secret commitments to foreign military alliances;
- Permitting or constructing foreign military infrastructure on Irish soil;
- Covert support for joint arms procurement or military R&D under EU/NATO auspices;
- Unauthorised military use of Irish civilian infrastructure (airports, ports, data centers).

Sanctions: High Court jurisdiction, fines, civil liability, and imprisonment (up to 10 years) depending on the severity and intent of the breach

3. Whistleblower Protection Provisions

Expanded legal protections are proposed for:

- Civil servants, contractors, or military personnel who expose violations of neutrality;
- Shielding against retaliation for reporting secretive or unconstitutional military cooperation;
- Criminalization of deliberate concealment of foreign military arrangements.

4. Creation of the Irish Neutrality and Sovereignty Commission (INSC)

An **independent constitutional watchdog body** tasked with safeguarding neutrality.

Composition: 12 members from civil society, academia, judiciary, military, and neutral international partners.

Mandate and Powers:

- Review treaties and defence agreements for neutrality compliance;
- Publish bi-annual **Neutrality Compliance Reports**;
- Issue **binding injunctions** and access classified material via **subpoena authority**;
- Trigger a **constitutional review** by the Supreme Court if neutrality is systemically endangered

5. Referendum Mechanism (Under Articles 46 and 47 of the Constitution)

Under Article 46, all constitutional changes regarding neutrality would be subject to a mandatory public referendum, ensuring that neutrality can only be altered by direct public consent.

Proposed constitutional safeguards include:

- Supermajority thresholds for change;
- Ban on automatic commitments without a referendum;
- Presumption of neutrality in legal interpretation unless clearly overridden by the people

6. National Economic Intelligence and Recovery Unit (NEIRU)

A proposed **economic oversight agency** to:

- Monitor threats from foreign economic coercion (e.g. tariffs, sanctions, investor pullouts);
- Prepare strategic responses to economic retaliation tied to neutrality policy;
- Strengthen **national economic sovereignty** through diversification and resilience planning

7. Cyber-Neutrality Safeguards and Digital Infrastructure Law

The book proposes a **Digital Geneva Initiative** to establish an international legal framework protecting civilian digital infrastructure in times of war and peace.

Domestic legal reforms would:

- Incorporate **cyberattacks into neutrality policy**;
- Mandate public and parliamentary oversight of **dual-use infrastructure** and **foreign digital surveillance cooperation**

8. Civil Reconstruction Authority (CRA)

In nuclear or hybrid warfare scenarios, the book proposes the creation of a **Civil Reconstruction Authority** to:

- Oversee post-crisis governance and humanitarian logistics;
- Prevent **emergency powers** from drifting into authoritarianism;
- Uphold **neutrality even in recovery governance**

Appendix K

Draft Referendum Bill – Irish Neutrality and Sovereignty Amendment

Short Title

This Act may be cited as the **Thirty-Ninth Amendment of the Constitution (Neutrality and Sovereignty) Bill**.

Bill Purpose

To propose an amendment to **Bunreacht na hÉireann** that enshrines Ireland's permanent military neutrality, prohibits participation in military alliances or foreign wars without a referendum, and establishes constitutional safeguards against indirect military entanglements.

Proposed Constitutional Amendment

The Constitution is hereby amended by the insertion of the following new Article after Article 29.9:

Article 29B – Irish Neutrality and Sovereignty

1. Ireland affirms its policy of **permanent, positive military neutrality**, rejecting participation in war, mutual defense alliances, and foreign military operations except as expressly permitted under this Constitution

2. Ireland shall not:

a) Join any military alliance, including NATO or a European Defense Union;
b) Host any foreign military bases, forces, or command structures on its territory;
c) Permit the use of its ports, airspace, infrastructure, or data systems for military purposes by foreign powers, except where expressly authorized under paragraph 3.

1. Military deployment of Irish Defense Forces abroad shall be permitted only where:

   a) Authorized by a resolution of the United Nations Security Council;
   b) Approved by the Government of Ireland; and
   c) Approved by a resolution of Dáil Éireann.

2. No international treaty, agreement, or legislative act shall override this Article without:

   a) A public referendum approved by a majority of the people; and
   b) an explanatory memorandum disclosing all military, intelligence, and economic implications.

3. The State shall establish an independent oversight commission to monitor compliance with this Article and report annually to the Oireachtas.

Transitional Provisions

- The Oireachtas shall review all existing agreements and treaty commitments inconsistent with Article 29B within twelve months of enactment.
- Ireland's participation in military structures under EU or NATO auspices shall cease unless re-authorized under the procedures set out in this Article.

Referendum Text (to appear on the ballot)

Proposal for a Constitutional Amendment:

Do you approve of the proposal to amend the Constitution to affirm Ireland's permanent military neutrality, prohibit participation in military alliances and foreign wars except where authorized by the United Nations and Dáil Éireann, and require a public referendum for any future military commitments?

[ ] Yes
[ ] No

Glossary of Terms

A

Alliance
A formal agreement between two or more states to cooperate on political, economic, or military matters, often to provide mutual security or support.

Anarchy (International Relations)
The condition of the international system lacking a central authority, which leads states to act in self-interest for survival, a core assumption in many IR theories.

Article 5 (NATO Treaty)
The mutual defense clause stating that an attack on one NATO member is considered an attack on all.

B

Bilateral
An agreement or relationship involving two countries only.

Borehole Wells
Deep wells drilled to access clean groundwater, vital in nuclear or climate emergencies.

C

Casualty Projections (Tiered)
Methodology for assessing direct, indirect, and long-term effects of warfare on a population.

Civic Engagement
Participation by citizens in political and social action, especially around neutrality and foreign policy.

Civil Defense
Organized, non-military measures taken to protect civilians in emergencies such as war or natural disasters.

Collective Security
A system in which nations agree that the security of one is the concern of all, and therefore commit to collective response against aggression.

Controlled-Environment Agriculture
Farming methods like hydroponics and greenhouses that shield crops from external contamination.

Customary International Law
International obligations arising from established state practice, rather than written treaties.

Cyber Neutrality
A doctrine proposing that a state's neutrality be extended to the cyber domain, prohibiting

participation in offensive cyber warfare and promoting digital sovereignty.

Cyber Warfare
The use of digital attacks—such as hacking, disinformation, or infrastructure sabotage—to damage, disrupt, or influence a nation's critical systems or political stability.

Cybercrime Act 2017 (Ireland)
Irish legislation aimed at combating online crimes, though not fully adapted to address state-level cyber threats.

D

Dáil Éireann
The lower house of the Irish parliament responsible for passing legislation and approving military deployments.

Digital Geneva Initiative
A proposed international framework to safeguard civilian digital infrastructure during times of cyber conflict, especially for neutral states.

Diplomacy
The practice of managing international relations through negotiation and dialogue rather than conflict.

Dual-Use Infrastructure
Facilities used for both civilian and military purposes, making them potential targets during war.

E

EEC (European Economic Community)
The precursor to the European Union, founded in 1957 to promote economic integration.

EEZ (Exclusive Economic Zone)
An area beyond and adjacent to the territorial sea, extending 200 nautical miles from the coast, over which a state has special rights regarding marine resources.

Export Diversification Strategy
A national plan to reduce economic dependency on a narrow set of trade partners or sectors, aimed at enhancing resilience and strategic independence.

F

Fallout (Nuclear)
Radioactive particles dispersed into the atmosphere after a nuclear explosion, potentially affecting distant regions.

Foreign Policy
A government's strategy in

dealing with other nations, encompassing diplomacy, trade, security, and international representation.

G

Geneva Conventions
International treaties setting standards for humanitarian treatment in war, including protection of civilians and POWs.

Geneva Conventions – Principle of Distinction
The rule requiring parties in armed conflict to distinguish between combatants and civilians and to target only the former.

H

Hague Convention V (1907)
An international treaty outlining the rights and duties of neutral powers during war.

Hybrid Warfare
A mix of conventional, irregular, cyber, and psychological tactics used to destabilize adversaries without open warfare.

I

Indirect Casualties
Deaths caused by secondary effects of war—such as infrastructure collapse, disease, and starvation.

Intelligence-Sharing Protocols
Agreements between countries or agencies to exchange classified information for mutual security, which may challenge neutrality if linked to military alliances.

International Law
A body of rules established by treaty or custom that governs the relations between states.

Irish Neutrality and Sovereignty Act (proposed)
A draft constitutional amendment aiming to formally enshrine Ireland's neutral status in law.

Iodine Tablets
Medical countermeasures used to protect the thyroid gland from radioactive iodine exposure.

J

Jus Cogens
Latin for "compelling law"; refers to peremptory norms of international law from which no derogation is permitted.

L

Law of the Sea (UNCLOS)
The international treaty defining maritime boundaries, including

rights over territorial seas and Exclusive Economic Zones (EEZs).

M

Microgrids
Localized energy systems that can operate independently from the main power grid.

Ministerial Orders
Administrative legal instruments issued by a government minister, often used in military operations under Irish law.

Multilateral
Involving more than two parties, typically through international institutions or collective agreements.

N

National Economic Intelligence and Recovery Unit (NEIRU)
A proposed Irish body to assess global economic threats, defend national economic sovereignty, and plan for post-crisis recovery.

NATO (North Atlantic Treaty Organization)
A military alliance formed in 1949 between North American and European countries for collective defense.

Neutrality
A policy position whereby a state abstains from participating in armed conflicts or military alliances.

NIS2 Directive (EU)
A cybersecurity law requiring EU member states to adopt stronger digital infrastructure protections, with implications for national sovereignty in cyber governance.

NPT (Treaty on the Non-Proliferation of Nuclear Weapons)
An international treaty aimed at preventing the spread of nuclear weapons and promoting peaceful uses of nuclear energy.

Nuclear Deterrence
The military strategy of preventing attack by the threat of retaliatory nuclear force.

P

Partnership for Peace (PfP)
A NATO programme that allows non-member countries to cooperate militarily with the alliance.

Peace Movement
A coalition of civil society actors advocating for disarmament and diplomacy.

Peacekeeping
The deployment of international forces (often by the UN) to maintain peace and security in conflict areas, typically with the consent of the parties involved.

PESCO (Permanent Structured Cooperation)
An EU framework for deeper defense cooperation among member states.

Public Awareness and Preparedness
Civic education and state initiatives to prepare the public for emergencies, including conflict.

R

Radiological Weapon (Dirty Bomb)
A device combining conventional explosives with radioactive material to contaminate areas and populations.

Referendum
A public vote on a specific issue—such as constitutional changes to protect neutrality.

Rendition Flights
The secretive transport of detainees by the U.S. and its allies, often bypassing legal protections.

Rome Statute
The founding treaty of the International Criminal Court (ICC), outlining war crimes and crimes of aggression.

Rules-Based International Order
The concept that global affairs should be governed by agreed-upon laws and norms rather than by power politics alone.

S

Selective Enforcement
Uneven application of laws, often criticized when international legal standards are applied inconsistently.

Soft Power
A country's ability to influence others through culture, values, and diplomacy rather than military force.

Sovereignty
The authority of a state to govern itself without external interference.

Strategic Geography
The consideration of a state's physical location as a factor in global security and military interest.

T

Tallinn Manual
A non-binding academic study that applies international law to cyber operations. Although influential, it lacks legal authority.

TPNW (Treaty on the Prohibition of Nuclear Weapons)
A binding international agreement that outlaws nuclear weapons under all circumstances.

Treaty
A legally binding formal agreement between states or international actors governed by international law.

Triple Lock
An Irish legal mechanism requiring three levels of approval—UN mandate, Government decision, and Dáil vote—before deploying troops abroad.

U

UNCLOS (United Nations Convention on the Law of the Sea)
A framework governing maritime conduct, including navigation rights, territorial waters, and undersea resources.

UN Charter – Article 2(4)
Prohibits the use of force in international relations unless in self-defense or with Security Council approval.

Undersea Cables
Submarine communications lines that carry internet and telecommunications data globally; strategically important for Ireland.

UNIFIL (United Nations Interim Force in Lebanon)
A long-standing UN peacekeeping mission in which Ireland has participated under the Triple Lock.

UN (United Nations)
An intergovernmental organization founded in 1945 to promote peace, security, and cooperation through its General Assembly, Security Council, and specialized agencies.

W

Weaponised Narratives
Media and messaging strategies designed to undermine public trust, promote division, or sway foreign opinion in times of conflict.

Index

A

abstention, 35, 80, 114
Abu, 208
accession, 29, 62
accessory, 76
accountability, 35, 39, 43, 46, 63, 68, 70, 72-75, 82, 138, 207, 209
accountable, 69, 74, 209
accusation, 61, 111
accusations, 59, 67, 72
Acquisitions, 176
acquitted, 56
actionable, 33
activism, 53-54, 56-57
Activists, 55, 187
activists, 188
activities, 5, 23, 47, 55, 68-69, 77, 193
activity, 22, 26, 87, 98, 149-150
actor, 4, 30, 50, 64, 69, 71, 73, 93, 104, 112, 114, 131, 166, 170, 172
actors, 33-34, 51, 55-56, 63, 82, 91, 95, 222, 224
acumen, 176
acute, 28, 158
acutely, 7
adaptability, 149
administration, 111, 118
adversarial, 87
adversaries, 2, 27, 32, 86-87, 156, 173, 221
Advocacy, 189
advocacy, 162, 188-189
AEConnect, 92
Afri, 187
afri, 188
Africa, 67, 113
aftermath, 8, 17, 40, 60, 203
afterthought, 148
agencies, 98, 221, 224

Agency, 22, 158
agency, 14, 31, 34, 100, 213
Agenda, 148
agenda, 78, 81-82, 106
agendas, 68, 83, 94, 127
aggression, 13, 27, 32-36, 43, 46, 59-61, 74, 79, 87, 108, 110-111, 168, 195, 203, 219, 223
Aggressor, 196
aggressor, 118, 196
agility, 135
agitation, 36
agreed defense, 223
agricultural, 156, 160
Agriculture, 219
agriculture, 151, 156, 159
agritech, 113
aircraft, 10, 20-21, 41-42, 46, 52, 64, 145, 149-150, 168, 192, 204
airfields, 166
Airport, 4, 19-20, 42, 46, 49, 52, 55, 85, 88, 119, 137, 165, 167, 173, 182, 187, 193, 207, 209
airport, 97
airports, 90, 139, 165-166, 209, 212
airspace, 10, 19-21, 23, 26, 40, 46, 85, 119, 124, 142, 161, 166, 203-204, 209, 211, 216
airstrike, 66
Airstrikes, 63
airstrikes, 59, 64
alarmism, 92
alarmist, 155
Alignment, 31, 36
alignment, 3-4, 9-14, 16, 26, 35, 40, 46, 49, 54, 57, 62, 75, 77, 79-82, 87-88, 90, 94-96, 98, 101, 103-105, 107-108, 121, 129-130, 140-141, 143-144, 151, 164, 171, 173, 193
alignments, 83, 115
allegations, 70, 208

allegiance, 46, 121
Alliance, 187, 219
alliance, 2, 9, 11, 15, 23, 29, 40, 42, 54, 59-70, 72-75, 77-78, 80, 86-90, 97, 100-101, 118, 121, 133, 141, 147-148, 161-162, 191, 209, 216, 222
alliances, 1, 5, 8, 11, 13, 18-19, 35-36, 42, 55, 66, 75, 79, 83, 92-94, 97, 101, 103-104, 115, 118-121, 123-127, 130, 135, 138, 142, 151-153, 164, 171, 180, 182, 196-197, 211-212, 215, 217, 221-222
ambassador, 10
Amendment, 211, 215, 217
amendment, 43, 49, 142, 212, 215, 221
AML, 175
ammunition, 69
Amnesty, 68
Amsterdam, 14
analysis, 4, 12, 24, 60, 110, 172-173, 177
analytical, 164, 175
Anarchy, 219
anew, 10
Anglo, 8
annexation, 33
annihilation, 161
annually, 108, 145, 216
anomaly, 96
anonymized, 28
apocalyptic, 155
apolitical, 132
apology, 72
appropriation, 22
approximately, 16, 108
aquifers, 146
Arab, 204
arbitration, 179
Arctic, 24-26, 97, 117-118, 120

arena, 32
armor, 71
arsenal, 33
arsenals, 146
Asia, 113, 132, 170
asterisk, 97
asymmetric, 32, 35, 53, 87
atmosphere, 158, 220
atrocities, 59, 64
attackers, 30
Attorney, 36
attribution, 28, 95
auspices, 139, 142, 200, 212, 217
austerity, 174
authorization, 161
authoritarian, 69
authoritarianism, 160, 214
autonomous, 88, 109, 148
autonomy, 8, 41, 80, 90, 105, 111, 118, 121, 126
availed, 110
aversion, 8

B

backbone, 1, 54, 180
Balkans, 71
ballot, 217
Baltic, 62
Baltics, 97
bandwidth, 100
Barack, 3
battalions, 95
battlefield, 3, 57, 170
battlefields, 145
battleground, 29
battlegrounds, 52
Battlegroups, 47
battlespace, 30
beacon, 2, 127

bedrock, 195
Belgrade, 64, 71
belligerent, 20
belligerents, 20, 27
beneficiaries, 97
Benghazi, 67-68
benign, 114
BEPS, 112
Bilateral, 219
bilateral, 21, 23, 35
biodegradable, 152
biodiversity, 146, 150-151
biological, 146
biomedicine, 113
Biopharma, 113
biosphere, 146
blackmail, 32
blackout, 157
blackouts, 169, 174
Blowback, 170
blueprint, 152
bombardments, 204
bombers, 145
bomblets, 71
border, 1, 13, 23-24, 46, 98, 132, 135
Borehole, 219
boreholes, 159
breadlines, 174
breadth, 175
Brexit, 23-24
Brigade, 16
Brigades, 16
Brinkmanship, 4
brokered, 104
brunt, 72
Brussels, 5, 18, 96, 109, 114
Budapest, 31
budgetary, 131, 140
buffered, 23
bulwarks, 81, 161

Bunreacht, 3, 55, 80, 90, 115, 138, 141, 143, 215
bureaucratic, 1, 35, 41, 57, 101, 144
bureaucrats, 97

C

Cabinet, 39
cabinet, 9
calculation, 17
calculus, 86, 130, 134
camouflage, 92
Campaign, 188
campaign, 30, 62, 64-65, 67, 70-73, 101, 111, 142, 156, 188, 199
campaigner, 189
cancer, 72, 158, 160, 167
capacities, 122
capacity, 21, 30, 41, 71, 98, 120, 123, 125, 143, 147-148, 157, 160, 165, 167
capita, 21
career, 175
careful, 14, 17
carefully, 33, 88, 119, 125, 127, 184
carrier, 150
carriers, 145
cartel, 75
cascading, 87, 169
Casualties, 166-167, 169-171, 221
casualties, 64, 66, 163-167, 170, 172-173, 203
CASUALTY, 163
Casualty, 219
casualty, 150, 168, 173
catastrophe, 151
catastrophic, 99-100
categories, 165
category, 35

Catholicism, 16
caveats, 89
celestial, 23
centric, 132
cereals, 156
cesium, 159
cessation, 142
CFSP, 14, 184
chaos, 64, 66-67, 159
chemically, 71
chronic, 167
chronically, 171
CIA, 68, 207-209
circumvention, 82
citizen, 94, 97, 208
citizens, 40, 43, 49, 51, 56, 94-95, 156, 219
Civic, 219, 223
civic, 36, 43, 51, 53, 55, 57, 101
Civilian, 64, 72, 100
civilian, 28, 31, 37, 59, 64, 66-68, 70-73, 78, 85-86, 89, 94-96, 98, 100, 105, 139, 146, 148, 164-169, 171-172, 185, 189, 203-205, 212, 214, 220
Civilians, 71
civilians, 4, 63, 66-67, 162, 174, 183, 203-204, 219, 221
civilization, 60
clandestine, 69
Clare Daly MEP, 189
classification, 34, 56
classified, 30, 140, 213, 221
cleansing, 62, 64, 70
clearance, 146
clergy, 16
clerical, 16
Climate, 24, 147-148
climate, 24-25, 75, 89, 93, 127, 146-152, 219
climate affected, 24

climates, 146
cloaked, 1, 64, 74, 92
cloaks, 92
CNBC, 176
CND, 188
CNN, 176
coalition, 31, 51, 75, 124, 168, 171, 222
coalitions, 116, 141
coastal, 21, 24, 146, 150, 173
codified, 12, 61, 80
codifies, 162
codify, 11, 31
Codifying, 123, 138, 143
coercive, 17, 31, 107, 115, 144
Cogens, 221
cogens, 43
cognitive, 36
coherence, 29, 122
coherent, 68
cohorts, 160
collaborate, 36, 99, 105
collaborating, 22
collaboration, 82, 88
collaborative, 78-79
Collateral, 165
collateral, 74, 152
collections, 176
colonial, 3, 7, 17, 50, 101, 143
colonialism, 13
colonized, 54
Combat, 149
combat, 41, 82, 88, 141, 211
combatant, 42, 81, 164, 172
combatants, 221
combating, 220
communication, 19-22, 31, 169
communications, 86, 91-92, 157, 167, 224
Communist, 16, 61
compass, 1, 80, 83, 103

compensation, 72
competition, 112, 118, 123
complicit, 209
complicity, 49, 69-70, 82, 112, 151, 188, 207, 209
component, 156
components, 42, 45, 167
Composition, 213
compromised, 15, 23, 97, 118, 160
compromising, 26, 200
compulsory, 12
concealment, 139, 212
concept, 2, 13, 28, 147, 149, 223
concessions, 11, 115
conclusion, 172
conclusive, 93
concrete, 16
condemnation, 70
condemned, 46, 59, 64
condemning, 69
conditionality, 110
condolences, 10
conduit, 75, 86
conferences, 176
confidence, 43, 131, 133, 143
confrontation, 13, 133, 135, 164
confrontational, 96
confrontations, 86
Congress, 12
connectivity, 99-100
conquer, 50
conscience, 2, 4, 56
conscientious, 188
consciousness, 42, 57
conscripted, 10
consensus, 8, 11, 41, 43, 47-48, 62, 73
consistency, 65
consistently, 4, 14, 129, 197
consortia, 93-94, 99

constellation, 7
constellations, 22
constitute, 33, 43, 139, 209
constitutes, 28
Constitution, 5, 17, 43, 80, 88, 90, 123, 134, 137-138, 141, 179-180, 188, 192-193, 211, 213, 215, 217
constitution, 12-13
Constitutionalising, 144
constitutionalising, 143
constitutionality, 141
constitutionally, 13, 24, 41
construction, 145
constructive, 142
consulates, 171
consultation, 43
consultations, 98
Consultative, 182
contaminants, 150
contaminate, 223
contaminated, 152, 156, 160
contaminates, 159
contamination, 72, 145-146, 158, 219
contemporaneous, 65
contentious, 65
continent, 19
continental, 8, 157
continents, 151
contingency, 110, 156
contingent, 184
continuity, 130, 133-134
continuously, 141
contraction, 172
contractors, 75, 97, 105, 139, 212
contravene, 73
contravening, 20
contribution, 79, 148
contributions, 79
contributor, 151
controversial, 63-65, 67, 72-75

controversies, 60
controversy, 47
Convention, 20-21, 31, 49, 55, 69, 71, 95, 98, 162, 183-185, 208-209, 221, 224
convention, 42
conventional, 27-28, 34, 86, 100, 122, 165, 167, 221, 223
Conventions, 20, 25-26, 49, 72-73, 82, 162, 183, 221
conventions, 183
convergence, 110, 143
conviction, 5, 116
convictions, 7
convoy, 65
convoys, 172
convulsing, 5
coordinated, 29, 87, 99, 109
coordinating, 31
Copenhagen, 118
Cork, 85, 97, 111, 114, 173, 175
corollary, 36
corporations, 4, 130
correspondence, 29
corroded, 104
Corrosion, 150
corrosive, 103, 111
counterbalance, 52
counterintelligence, 31
countermeasures, 86, 114, 221
counterpoint, 16
courage, 2, 83, 103, 116
coverage, 99
Covert, 139, 212
covert, 26, 32, 36, 68, 87, 93, 126, 207
CRA, 160, 214
crafted, 98
Creation, 212
creation, 8, 34, 115, 140, 214
credentials, 89, 105

credibility, 48, 50, 55, 64, 68, 71, 74-75, 83, 105
Crimea, 33
criminalise, 138
Criminalization, 212
criminalize, 56, 212
criminalizes, 56
crises, 25, 48, 62, 65, 152, 172
crisis, 14, 21, 29, 31, 35-36, 47, 50, 68, 77, 92, 115, 148, 156, 159, 163, 173, 214, 222
criteria, 49
Critical, 31
critical, 19, 29, 36, 56, 79, 86, 91, 93, 117, 120, 122, 124, 126, 129, 133, 151, 156, 158, 161, 177, 199, 220
critically, 205
criticism, 10, 63, 66, 71, 189
Critics, 42, 68, 78, 205
critics, 14, 41, 47, 59, 63, 103
critiquing, 55
crossfire, 4
crosshairs, 107
crossover, 166
CROSSROADS, 2-83, 85-178, 180-224
Crossroads, 177
crossroads, 1, 82, 126
Crucially, 31
crucially, 81
crucible, 15
cruise, 167
crumbling, 3
crystallized, 8
CSDP, 12, 23
CTF, 175
culminating, 63, 65
culprits, 93
cultivate, 122, 131
cultivated, 50

cultivating, 127
cumulative, 17, 146, 172
curating, 176
currency, 3, 33
Cyber, 27-29, 31, 34, 86, 169, 214, 219-220
cyber, 18, 22, 28-35, 86, 88, 94, 120, 123-124, 131, 133, 165, 168, 170, 173, 185, 219-222, 224
cyberattack, 28, 30, 97, 167
Cyberattacks, 27, 33, 53
cyberattacks, 20, 28-29, 33-34, 79, 95, 169, 214
Cybercrime, 29, 31, 185, 220
cybercrime, 56
cybercriminals, 30
CYBERSECURITY, 27
Cybersecurity, 122, 124
cybersecurity, 20, 22, 28-29, 31, 36, 54, 98, 148, 185, 193, 222
Cyberspace, 31
cyberspace, 3, 27, 29-30
cyberwarfare, 3

D

Dáil, 39-42, 45-46, 81, 138, 199, 201, 216-217, 220, 224
dairy, 113, 156
Daly, 189
darkness, 157, 169
daylight, 103
DCU, 189
deadlier, 174
debris, 158
decarbonize, 146
December, 208
decentralised, 157, 160
decentralize, 43
decentralized, 57
decisive, 130

declassified, 61
decolonization, 11
decommissioned, 150
decontamination, 158-159
dedication, 11, 127
deepwater, 88
defects, 167
Defence, 12, 14, 21-23, 34, 42, 79-80, 82, 109, 149, 152, 165, 172, 192, 196
defence, 21-25, 28-29, 31, 33, 36, 137-144, 147-152, 156-157, 161, 164, 166, 168-174, 180, 191, 193, 196, 213
defences, 165
defendants, 56
defender, 16, 55, 153
Defenders, 56
defenders, 59
Defense, 14, 87, 124, 133, 145, 216, 219
defense, 4-5, 11, 13-15, 17-18, 41, 43, 47, 50-52, 55-56, 59-60, 62, 65, 73-75, 77-83, 86-89, 91-97, 103, 105, 108-110, 115, 118-122, 124, 126, 131, 133-135, 146, 183-185, 188, 191, 193, 197, 215, 219, 222, 224
defensive, 8, 17, 20, 51, 62, 67, 124
deficits, 55
deforestation, 146
degradation, 27, 145-146, 149, 173
degrade, 32, 146
degraded, 169
dehydration, 167
deliberately, 40, 127
delivery, 169
demilitarised, 151
demilitarization, 56, 200

democracies, 62, 88
democracy, 10, 43, 60-61, 103-104, 125, 143
democratic, 2, 29, 32, 36, 39-41, 43, 46-47, 52, 57, 59, 63, 66, 71, 82, 93, 101, 103, 122, 143-144, 152, 187, 201, 205
democratically, 138
demonstrations, 45
Denmark, 25, 117-121, 125-126
denominator, 172
densely, 164-165
departure, 16, 79
dependence, 71, 89, 114, 160, 173
depleted, 63-64, 71, 146
deployed, 22, 24, 27, 71, 82, 109, 195, 200
deploying, 32, 42, 49, 224
Deployment, 200
deployment, 25, 39-40, 42-43, 45-46, 65, 72, 81, 85, 115, 129, 145, 161, 196, 199-200, 205, 216, 223
deployments, 46-47, 50, 72, 100, 135, 147, 151, 199, 220
depopulation, 160
deprivation, 69
derogation, 221
designated, 108
destabilisation, 29, 33
destabilize, 221
destabilizing, 87
destination, 96, 167
destinations, 129
destiny, 125
detached, 112, 163
detachment, 35
detained, 208
detainee, 67
detainees, 68-69, 223
detection, 86, 96, 99, 158
detention, 68-69, 207-209

detentions, 68
DETER, 129
deteriorate, 167
determination, 7, 9, 121, 126, 179
Deterrence, 222
deterrence, 86, 88, 95, 100, 148, 152, 168
deterrent, 12, 59, 61, 74, 89, 108, 155
deterring, 71
deters, 124
detonation, 158, 168
devastated, 75, 146, 160
devastation, 159, 165
deviation, 139
device, 223
devices, 169
Devine, 189
devotion, 179
diaspora, 112
diffuse, 125
diffused, 63
Digitally, 56
digitally, 30
dignity, 112, 208-209
dilemma, 101
diligence, 175-176
dilute, 92
dilution, 184
Diplomacy, 113, 220
diplomacy, 1-2, 12-14, 30-32, 48, 55, 64, 74-75, 79, 88, 90, 92-93, 102, 104, 107, 113, 123, 126, 140, 144, 152, 155, 160, 164, 221-223
diplomatic, 10-12, 15, 17, 29, 41, 52, 54, 66, 75, 79, 87, 89, 92, 95, 97-98, 108, 115, 117, 119, 121-122, 127, 130-132, 134, 137, 142, 162, 171-173
Diplomatically, 88

diplomatically, 28, 33, 37, 71, 83, 111, 119
diplomats, 10, 181
Directive, 31, 82, 185, 222
directly, 17, 32, 82, 112, 133, 143, 150, 168, 195
disadvantage, 156
Disarmament, 188
disarmament, 11, 13, 127, 149, 162, 222
disaster, 77, 89, 148, 152, 157, 173
disasters, 219
discard, 101
discernment, 46
disclaimed, 68
disclosing, 216
disclosure, 139
discomfort, 40
discourse, 2, 14, 93-94, 101, 124, 127, 155
discretion, 30, 39, 56, 80, 82, 135, 137
discretionary, 89
disease, 101, 165, 168, 221
disengagement, 66
disfigurement, 72
disinformation, 29, 32-34, 36, 87, 125, 144, 220
disinvestment, 111
dismantle, 81, 103
dismantled, 43, 82
dismantlement, 42
dismantling, 43
disorder, 5, 74
disperse, 71
displaced, 70, 172
displacement, 24, 149, 164-165, 171
disproportionate, 82, 86, 113-114
disrupt, 132, 146, 165, 171, 220

disrupted, 168
disrupting, 30, 86, 150
Disruption, 171
disruption, 24-25, 27-28, 32, 34, 56, 69, 97, 99, 108, 151, 167
Disruptions, 93, 130
disruptions, 167
disruptive, 56
dissected, 3
dissecting, 45
dissent, 2, 55-57, 103
distant, 7, 53, 117, 126, 151, 168, 172, 209, 220
distillation, 159
Distinction, 221
distinction, 43, 46, 63, 78, 162, 200
distinctive, 79
distinctiveness, 12
disturbances, 150-151
diverge, 126
divergence, 23, 192
divergent, 23, 62
divers, 93
Diversification, 113, 115, 124, 220
diversification, 213
diversified, 113
Diversifying, 122
diversifying, 120
dividend, 147
divisiveness, 7
Djakovica, 65
doctrinal, 29
doctrine, 3, 7, 17, 25, 29-30, 35-36, 53, 65, 73, 78, 80, 86, 114-115, 161, 164, 166, 219
doctrines, 28, 60, 72
documentaries, 57
dogma, 53
Domestically, 113, 127

domestically, 13, 16, 159
dominance, 78, 120
domination, 2, 17, 53
Donald, 2, 107, 117
Donegal, 10
dozens, 64, 66, 99, 171
DPO, 188
dramatically, 86, 157, 173
drastically, 158
drifting, 2, 47, 214
Dual, 220
dual, 12-13, 22-23, 148, 165, 167, 214
duality, 59
Duffy, 16
durable, 74, 100
Duties, 20
duties, 162, 221
duty, 96

E

Éamon, 9, 16, 181
earlywarning, 95
earthquakes, 93
easily, 36, 94, 104, 127, 131
Eastern, 19, 86, 171
ECHR, 55, 207-209
ecological, 146-147, 149, 151
ecologically, 146
ecology, 149, 151
Economically, 26, 90, 110
economically, 105, 111, 132-133
ecosystem, 99, 152, 168
ecosystems, 29, 146, 149-150
EctHR, 57
EDA, 22
EDF, 79-81, 109
Edmund, 5

education, 48, 52, 54, 66, 125, 129, 131, 133, 140, 156, 171, 175-176, 223
educational, 36
educators, 57
EEC, 14-15, 182, 184, 220
eerie, 155
EEZ, 21, 151, 184, 220
EEZs, 222
effectively, 94, 121, 126, 192, 205
effectiveness, 62, 148, 159
efficiency, 147
Einstein, 2
Éireann, 39, 45, 81, 138, 201, 216-217, 220
electricity, 98, 157, 167
elevation, 86, 88
elite, 4
elites, 43, 105
elusive, 95
emails, 104
embargo, 204
Embassies, 171
embassies, 97, 112
embedded, 17, 31, 42, 87, 113
embedding, 43, 141, 143
embroiled, 7
emergencies, 219, 223
Emergency, 3, 9-12, 158, 165, 181
emergency, 4, 21-22, 26, 35, 99-100, 147-148, 157, 159-160, 169, 171, 173, 214
emergent, 57
Emerson, 3
emission, 147
emissions, 145-152
emits, 145
emphasis, 155, 166
empire, 2
empires, 5, 96

employment, 113
empowered, 43
empowering, 5, 113
emptive, 34, 161, 166
ENAAT, 188
enaat, 188
enacted, 36, 180
enactment, 216
encrypted, 29, 36, 92, 95
encryption, 31
endless, 52
enduring, 8, 57, 63, 72, 123, 138, 143
Energy, 157
energy, 21, 25, 29, 31, 33, 100, 132, 145, 150, 157, 160, 172-173, 222
enforceable, 30-31, 73, 138-139
Enforcement, 36, 212, 223
enforcement, 21-22, 30, 43, 73, 98, 138, 140, 184, 196, 199, 203
Engagement, 219
engagement, 20, 35, 40, 43, 47, 50-51, 57, 67-68, 73-74, 81, 123, 125-127, 130, 134, 137, 140, 172, 182, 196, 201
engagements, 49
enlargement, 192
enriched, 175
enshrine, 5, 90, 211, 221
enshrined, 12-13, 24, 43, 115, 127, 205
enshrinement, 138
enshrines, 161, 215
enshrining, 152
entail, 103
entails, 20, 79
entangled, 75, 92-93, 132-133
entanglement, 2, 11, 15, 22-23, 26, 39, 77, 79-80, 95, 103, 105, 108, 143
entanglements, 7-8, 126, 129, 134, 162, 170, 215
entangling, 18
entirely, 132, 146, 149, 156-157, 169
entrants, 131
entrapment, 105
entrenched, 12
ENVIRONMENTAL, 145
Environmental, 158
environmental, 21, 25-26, 52, 65, 72, 145-149, 151-152
environmentalism, 54
environmentally, 100, 152
Eoin, 16
EPA, 158
episode, 16
episodes, 66
equipment, 158
equity, 132
Era, 181
era, 2-3, 52, 61, 107, 121, 134
erased, 164
Erosion, 112
erosion, 3, 21, 42, 46, 57, 101, 103, 109, 137, 143
erratic, 172
eruption, 100
Es Revellar Art Resort, 176
escalate, 8, 172
escalates, 40, 169
escalating, 64, 86, 108
escalation, 11, 31, 66, 102, 168-169
ESDP, 14
espionage, 27, 29, 95
establishment, 73, 139
Estonia, 33
Ethically, 63
ethics, 5
euro, 108

evacuation, 66, 89, 156
evacuations, 158
evident, 157
evolution, 72
exacerbate, 145
examination, 91
Excerpts, 204
exclusion, 11
exclusively, 22
executed, 28, 64
exemplifies, 45
exempt, 146, 150
exert, 27
exerted, 123
exerts, 118, 191
existential, 35, 61, 75, 153, 157, 159
expanse, 117
expansion, 60-62, 113, 188
expansions, 135
expansively, 67
expectation, 143
expectations, 109, 115, 131
expedience, 70
expediency, 42, 105, 125
expel, 181
expendable, 108
expenditure, 32, 131
expenditures, 66
expertise, 175-176
explanatory, 216
Explicitly, 204
explicitly, 14, 57, 63, 108, 115, 199
exploitable, 32
exploitation, 33
exploited, 20-21, 115
exploiting, 29, 62
exploration, 25
explosion, 220
exponentially, 168

exporter, 156
export-oriented, 160
exposure, 17, 24, 28, 86, 101, 114, 131, 134, 158, 164, 167, 221
expression, 18, 39, 55-56, 80, 102
expressions, 53
expressly, 80, 142, 215-216
extensive, 146, 176
externally, 66
extraordinary, 68, 145, 207, 209
extremist, 69

F

Facebook, 168
facility, 169
faction, 75
factions, 67-68, 71
facto, 15, 19, 63, 121, 141, 151
factories, 64
fairness, 112
faith, 103
fallback, 157
Fallout, 158, 169, 171, 220
fallout, 4, 157-159, 165, 167
Fallujah, 72
Farmers, 160
farmers, 51
Fascist, 16
fatalities, 165
fate, 2, 42, 144
favorable, 93, 130
favoritism, 110
FDI, 130
feasible, 100, 106
feet, 113
Fertiliser, 159
fertilisers, 156
fervor, 41
Fewer, 94
fewer, 21, 165

fiction, 164
field-tested, 33
fiercely, 106
fighter, 32, 145, 149
Fine Art Transactions, 176
Finlandization, 13
fintech, 132
firepower, 75, 89
firewall, 39
firmly, 11, 14
fiscal, 109, 115, 133
fisheries, 26, 150-151
fissures, 114
flair, 92
flashpoint, 42, 61
flashpoints, 3
flawed, 66
fleet, 1, 99
fluctuating, 66
fluid, 17, 35
focal, 119, 123
Forbes, 176
forensic, 34, 64
fortified, 37
fortifying, 127
fortress, 134
fossil, 145, 149, 157
Foundation, 200
foundation, 29, 35, 39, 48, 59, 109, 125, 143, 162, 183
foundational, 7, 69, 80, 127, 191, 197, 199
foundations, 123
Foynes, 85
fractured, 10, 50, 68, 83, 114
Franco, 15-16
fratricidal, 8
freedom, 9, 54-55, 60, 130, 149
freedoms, 102
freely, 106
friction, 15, 41, 88, 132, 171

fringe, 51, 105
frontline, 34, 79, 110, 132
fulfill, 89
fully, 17, 45, 112, 121, 127, 220
functionality, 50, 160
fundamentally, 61, 69, 118, 126, 134
furthered, 175

G

Gaddafi, 63, 67, 203, 205
Galway, 57, 97, 173
garb, 92
gateway, 77, 132, 201
GDP, 108, 131
geiger, 158
genetic, 158
genocide, 142
genuine, 47, 64
geographic, 9, 85, 89, 96, 166, 170
geographical, 19, 61
geographically, 12, 23
Geography, 223
geography, 164, 166
geolocation, 22
GEOPOLITICAL, 19
geopolitical, 1, 19-20, 22-24, 26, 28-29, 31, 34, 40, 45, 59, 62, 64, 82, 86, 92, 94, 96, 100-101, 109, 113, 115, 117-119, 130-133, 138, 147, 150-151, 191, 193
geopolitically, 27
geopolitics, 25, 75, 92, 112, 114
geostrategic, 4
gland, 221
glaring, 109
globalized, 114
globally, 48, 97, 105, 143, 169, 224

Glossary, 219
goal, 27, 52, 96
Goals, 147
goals, 71, 74, 77-78, 110, 193
Golan, 3
goodwill, 119, 132
Gorge, 65
Governance, 160
governance, 39, 66, 71, 78, 112, 116, 120, 130, 141, 157, 159, 214, 222
Government, 40, 42-43, 45, 138, 142, 157, 179-180, 192, 199, 201, 216, 224
government, 5, 9-11, 15-16, 19, 23, 33, 36, 41, 46-47, 52, 55, 57, 65-68, 77-78, 81, 91-92, 98-100, 102-103, 110, 112-113, 123, 127, 140-141, 156-157, 159, 167, 180, 220, 222
governmental, 15, 23
Governments, 93
governments, 11, 24, 32, 42, 47, 49, 75, 102, 105, 144, 150, 191
grains, 156
grassroots, 53, 187
Grdelica, 65
greenhouse, 145, 150
greenhouses, 159, 219
GREENLAND, 117
Greenland, 117-123, 125-127
Greenlandic, 118, 121
Greenwashing, 148
groundwater, 159, 219
groundwork, 17, 118, 184
GTT, 92
Guantanamo, 208
guarantor, 125
guardian, 140
guardianship, 57
guidance, 158

guidelines, 30, 71, 161
guise, 40, 79, 111, 121, 160
guises, 70

H

habitable, 24
habitat, 150
habitats, 146
Hague, 20, 26, 49, 162, 183, 221
hallmark, 96
hallmarks, 30
Handbook, 176
hard-fought, 1
hardship, 2
harmful, 146, 150
harmonization, 82
harmonized, 109
haste, 40
headlines, 48, 107, 151
headquartered, 28, 86
headquarters, 168
healthcare, 31, 34, 159-160, 171
Heights, 3
hÉireann, 3, 55, 80, 90, 115, 138, 141, 143, 215
hereby, 215
heritage, 60
HERO, 59
hesitation, 32
Hibernia, 92
hierarchy, 121
high-ranking, 47
highways, 92
hinge, 143, 157
hinted, 117
historic, 155
historical, 5, 7, 12-13, 17, 53, 81, 121, 164
Historically, 19, 32, 172

historically, 13, 54, 79-80, 88, 156, 171-173
Hitler, 10
hoc, 35
holistic, 148
homegrown, 113
honesty, 55, 103
horizon, 1
hostile, 36, 91
hostility, 61, 70, 89, 172
Hotel, 176
Household, 176
households, 171
Humanitarian, 171, 211
humanitarian, 4, 13, 24, 41, 46, 48-50, 52, 60-65, 67-68, 71, 73, 77, 82, 88, 92, 104, 138-139, 142, 144, 147, 149, 161-162, 170, 172, 182-183, 185, 200-201, 203-205, 214, 221
humanitarianism, 13
humanity, 53, 184
Hungary, 62
hunger, 113
hurdle, 39
HYBRID, 27
Hybrid, 32, 34, 95, 221
hybrid, 3, 18, 20, 30, 32-37, 41, 79, 83, 95, 122, 214
hydroponic, 159
hydroponics, 219
hyperscale, 133

I

IAWM, 188
ICC, 223
Iceland, 25
icy, 117
ideological, 7-8, 10, 16, 41, 53, 60
ideology, 15

IHL, 71-72
illegitimate, 196
illicit, 70
imminent, 79
immune, 151, 155, 170, 173
immunity, 49, 63, 73, 107
impartiality, 89
impediment, 41
imperative, 42, 63, 102
implementation, 204
imported, 156-157, 159
importing, 8, 149
imprisonment, 139, 212
improvised, 35
impunity, 33, 70
inability, 70
inaction, 65
inadmissible, 69
incentive, 87
incentives, 113, 133
incident, 31, 64, 159, 171
incidents, 27, 35
incommunicado, 208
incursions, 21, 28, 30, 33, 124
indigenous, 124
indiscriminate, 72-73, 82, 162
inefficient, 146
inertia, 5
inference, 104
inflation, 101, 170-171
inflicted, 111
influential, 28, 224
influx, 165
infographics, 54
infrastructural, 88, 170
Infrastructure, 31, 104, 169, 171, 214, 220
infrastructure, 4, 20-21, 23, 27-31, 33-36, 56, 63-64, 66, 75, 79, 82, 86-87, 89, 91, 93-101, 103, 105-106, 108, 111, 113, 118-119,

122, 124, 126, 130-134, 138-139, 141, 145, 148, 157-160, 162-163, 165-170, 172-173, 189, 204, 211-212, 214, 216, 220-222
infringe, 5
infringing, 56, 140
inherently, 53, 147, 164
Initiative, 31, 214, 220
initiative, 36, 79, 184
initiatives, 18, 22-23, 88, 137, 148, 176, 223
injunctions, 140, 213
injury, 28, 72, 162
innocence, 104
innovate, 149
innovation, 22, 101, 112, 122, 129-133, 135, 148
innovative, 48
INSC, 140, 142, 212
insecurity, 149
insertion, 215
insight, 125, 175
insights, 176-177
insinuation, 93
installation, 87
instinctive, 7
institution, 141, 196
institutional, 30, 39, 57, 69, 73, 103, 138, 140, 145, 150, 161
institutionalized, 125
institutionally, 163
institutions, 29, 32, 34, 36, 66, 68, 80, 88, 110, 112, 126, 134, 138, 160, 175, 222
instructive, 47
instrumental, 29
insular, 166
insulated, 129
insulates, 63
insulation, 75, 130-131
insurgency, 65

insurgents, 66
integrate, 81
integrated, 31, 85, 87, 158, 166, 168
integrates, 110
integration, 1, 11, 14-15, 17, 23, 29, 41, 47, 77-80, 102, 108-109, 114, 143, 172, 184, 197, 220
integrity, 21, 43, 47, 69, 88, 103-104, 127, 195, 200
intellectual, 109, 129
Intelligence, 85, 110, 115, 213, 221-222
intelligence, 5, 10, 27, 30-31, 34, 36, 47, 52, 65-66, 69, 85, 87-88, 95-96, 124, 148, 162, 166, 169, 209, 216
intelligence sharing, 138
intense, 71
intensify, 82
intensive, 145, 147
intention, 5
intentional, 98
intentioned, 205
interactive, 54
interconnected, 157
interconnectors, 157
interdependence, 82, 166
interference, 12, 29, 33, 56, 87, 122, 124, 223
intergovernmental, 224
Interim, 45, 224
interlinked, 165
Internally, 62
internationalism, 36
Internationally, 36, 56
internationally, 31, 33, 46, 123
Internet, 99
internet, 20, 86, 91, 93, 97, 103, 169, 224
interoperability, 79, 147, 192

interpretation, 10, 47-48, 56, 63, 74, 80, 205, 213
interred, 10
interrogation, 68
interruption, 157
interruptions, 99
intersection, 120
intertwined, 147, 151
Intervention, 15
intervention, 30, 34, 60, 63-68, 73, 79, 81, 121, 196, 203, 205
interventionism, 53
interventionist, 74, 188
interventions, 32, 59-60, 62-65, 67-68, 71, 74, 138, 192, 200, 211
INTRODUCTION, 1
introduction, 40
intrusion, 86
intrusions, 28, 86
invalidate, 180
invaluable, 100
invasion, 9, 13, 41, 46, 182
invasions, 28, 32, 40
inversion, 96
investigation, 64, 208
Investigations, 63, 68, 207
investigations, 175
investigative, 68
INVESTMENT, 129
Investment, 124, 157
investment, 11, 87-88, 90, 101, 108, 111, 113-114, 124-125, 129, 131-134, 170, 176
investments, 35, 112, 118, 132, 135
investor, 130-131, 135, 143, 176, 213
Investors, 130, 133
investors, 129, 132-135, 175
iodide, 158
IRA, 16

IRELAND, 2-83, 85-178, 180-224
Ireland, 1-5, 7-32, 34-37, 39-43, 45-56, 74-83, 85-116, 119-127, 129-135, 137-138, 140-144, 147-153, 155-175, 177, 179-185, 187-188, 191-193, 195-197, 199-201, 203, 205, 207, 209, 212, 215-217, 220-221, 224
irg, 188
Irish-American, 111
ISAF, 65
isolationism, 12
isolationist, 83

J

Jamahiriya, 204
jeopardize, 119
jet, 149
jets, 32, 145
jihadist, 67, 171
journalism, 36
journalists, 68
Judgment, 208
judgment, 104
judicial, 43, 49, 56, 63, 139, 179
judiciary, 56, 140, 213
junior, 106
jurisdiction, 139, 212
jurisdictions, 27
Justice, 56
justice, 5, 41, 48, 55, 69, 71, 74-75, 111, 116, 147, 179, 188
justification, 43, 73, 91, 103
justifications, 59-60, 63, 68

K

Keep Ireland Out, 54
Kennedy, 1

Kerry, 94
keynote, 176
keystone, 48
KFOR, 65, 70-71, 199-200
Khaled, 208
kilometers, 94
Kinetic, 169
kinetic, 33, 35, 169, 172-173
Kingdom, 11, 21, 23
KLA, 70
Kosovar, 64
Kunduz, 66
KYC, 175
Kyoto, 146, 150

L

labs, 133
Lancashire, 175
landmark, 201
landmass, 85
landmines, 71
Lannon, 189
latency, 100
launched, 28, 64, 67, 72, 173, 204, 207
launching, 22
lawfare, 3
lawful, 35, 41, 43, 49, 73-74, 184, 196, 200
lawfully, 56
leaching, 150
leader, 123
leaders, 7-8, 57, 61, 103, 130
leadership, 11, 70, 96, 100, 103, 114, 116, 118, 121, 143, 149
League, 187
leftist, 15, 53
leftover, 102
legality, 39, 43, 56, 62, 70, 73, 112, 205

Legally, 35, 42, 90
legally, 12, 28, 31, 37, 40, 43, 59, 65, 69, 109, 115, 121, 139, 161-162, 209, 224
legislation, 23, 30-31, 35-36, 43, 54, 56, 102, 185, 220
legislative, 26, 29, 49, 83, 216
legislators, 112
legitimacy, 41, 43, 46, 48-49, 61-62, 65-66, 68-70, 74, 141, 143, 173, 195, 197, 199, 201
legitimate, 45, 86, 90, 138, 166, 173
legitimately, 73
legitimize, 11
legitimizes, 196
legitimizing, 199
length, 80
lens, 16, 105, 145
LEO, 100
liability, 32, 72, 134, 137, 139, 209, 212
liable, 43
Liberation, 70, 107
liberator, 75
libraries, 52
lieu, 196
lifeblood, 46
lifelines, 94
lifespan, 141
lifestyle, 54
lighthouse, 134
likelihood, 95, 101, 118, 173
limitation, 142
limitations, 16, 126, 165
limitless, 120
linchpin, 20, 117
Lisbon, 15, 17, 81, 110, 182, 184
literacy, 36
litmus, 46
litres, 149-150

LLB, 175
LLM, 175
lobbies, 144
lobbying, 5, 122, 125, 188
Localized, 222
logistical, 19, 26, 40, 46, 79, 81-82, 85, 88, 104, 139, 162
logistically, 133, 162
Logistics, 113
logistics, 4, 20, 49, 85, 88-89, 132, 147, 162, 165-167, 169, 193, 214
longer, 23, 54, 61, 75, 86, 88, 90, 92, 101, 104, 106-108, 115, 117, 125, 127, 135, 147, 157, 163-164, 170, 172
longest, 67
loophole, 46, 49, 146
loopholes, 3, 5
loyalty, 209
lurking, 94
Luther, 4
Lutnick, 109
luxury, 18

M

Maastricht, 14, 184
machinery, 40, 57
Magazine, 176
magnet, 134
magnitude, 101
mainland, 167
maintenance, 85, 95, 98, 145
majority, 43, 93, 216
malice, 99
mammal, 150
manageable, 100
management, 14, 42, 77, 100, 124
Mandate, 199, 213-214

mandate, 31, 34, 40, 43, 57, 61, 63, 65, 67, 70, 74, 109-110, 137, 142, 161, 201, 205, 224
mandated, 13, 46, 108, 138, 200, 211
mandates, 24, 43, 73-74, 81, 184, 188, 192, 205
mandating, 185
mandatory, 213
manipulated, 36, 101
manipulation, 32-33, 101, 123-124, 126, 143
manner, 195
manufacturers, 75, 131
map, 158
marginalized, 110
margins, 75
Marxist, 16
masquerading, 1
Masri, 208
materializes, 127
materiel, 89
meaningful, 30, 70, 133, 156
meaningless, 111
meat, 156
Mechanism, 213
mechanism, 40, 42, 48-49, 51, 78, 81, 141, 180, 195-197, 199, 211, 224
Mechanisms, 211
mechanisms, 30, 35, 73, 80-82, 98, 110, 114
mediate, 83, 105
mediation, 79
mediator, 12, 18
medication, 169
mediumsized, 145
membership, 11, 13-14, 62, 78, 86-90, 94-95, 97, 102, 105, 108-109, 115, 130-134, 137, 142, 161, 163, 168, 182, 192-193, 196

memes, 57
memorandum, 216
MEP, 189
merely, 8, 17-18, 42, 53-54, 59, 62, 64, 82-83, 89, 102-103, 106, 117, 139, 142-143, 147, 157
mesh, 99
Meta, 93, 130, 168
metal, 150
metals, 146
Methodology, 219
methodology, 164, 166
methods, 32, 219
microgrid, 157
Microgrids, 222
Microsoft, 93, 168
Militarily, 90
militarily, 25, 40, 52, 61, 75, 83, 91, 132, 138, 162, 166, 205, 222
Militarisation, 151
militarisation, 78, 153
militarised, 151, 153, 166
militarism, 8, 52, 76, 137, 188, 196
MILITARIZATION, 145
Militarization, 3, 132, 145, 147
militarization, 23, 26, 54, 90, 106, 146-147, 151, 188-189
militarize, 104, 106, 131
militarized, 21-22, 25, 46, 59, 105
militarizing, 101
militias, 67
Milošević, 64
minimum, 112
Ministerial, 222
ministerial, 42
Ministry, 30
minorities, 70
missile, 22, 25, 86, 165, 169, 173
missiles, 135, 167

mission, 40-41, 45-46, 48, 63, 65-67, 74, 78, 200, 224
Missions, 49-50
missions, 3, 11, 24-26, 41, 45, 48-49, 53, 75, 77, 82, 93, 104, 113, 138, 142, 147-148, 182, 184, 188, 201
mitigated, 93
mitigation, 146
mobilisation, 157, 165
mobility, 89
mobilize, 83
modernity, 51
modernization, 87, 98
modernize, 47
Modigliani, 177
momentum, 57
MONUC, 49
monument, 33
mood, 16
morality, 64, 179
morally, 47, 65
mortality, 167, 171
Moscow, 163
motive, 95-96
motives, 62, 65
MOVEMENT, 51
Movement, 4, 188, 222
movement, 51-57, 62
movements, 118
MSD, 130
Muammar, 63, 67, 203
multi, 108, 172
multidisciplinary, 34
multifaceted, 175
Multilateral, 98, 222
multilateral, 11, 13, 46-48, 122, 196, 205
multilateralism, 104
multilaterally, 40
multilayered, 49

multinational, 4, 27, 47, 93, 129, 131, 134, 147
multinationals, 112
Multiple, 99
multiple, 4, 90, 120, 156, 165, 175
multiplier, 24
multipolar, 120
municipal, 158
Munitions, 71, 185
munitions, 63-64, 71-72, 146, 185
murals, 53, 57
murky, 32, 95
Museum, 176
mutually, 50, 113
Myth, 111
myth, 107, 112
mythology, 55

N

naïveté, 2
namely, 55, 69
Narrative, 111
narrative, 16, 91-94, 96, 98, 102, 111-112
Narratives, 224
narratives, 94, 97, 112, 143
narrowly, 47
nascent, 22
Nashiri, 208
Nationalists, 15-16
nationally, 167
NATO, 2, 4, 10-14, 18-21, 23-26, 29, 31, 33, 36, 40, 47, 55, 59-81, 85-91, 94-103, 105-110, 115, 118-119, 121, 123, 129-135, 137, 139, 143-144, 147-148, 150-152, 155-156, 158, 161-164, 166-174, 181-184, 187-189, 191-193, 197, 199-200, 203-205, 212, 216-217, 219, 222

NATOaffiliated, 171
NATOaligned, 80
NATOled, 65
nautical, 21, 220
Naval, 146, 150
naval, 21, 85, 98, 147, 149-151
navies, 93
navigating, 70, 175
navigation, 22, 150, 224
NCSC, 28
negligence, 159
negligently, 138
negotiation, 3, 17, 220
negotiations, 14
NEIRU, 110-111, 213, 222
Netflix, 92
NeutralIreland, 54
NEUTRALITY, 2-83, 85-178, 180-224
Neutrality, 1, 4-5, 18, 22, 24, 35-36, 53, 55, 79, 83, 89, 101, 104, 110, 115-116, 119, 123, 135, 138, 140-141, 143-144, 147, 149, 152, 160, 166, 173, 177, 179, 181, 187-188, 191, 195, 205, 209, 211-215, 219, 221-222
neutrality, 2-5, 7-32, 34-37, 39-40, 42-43, 46-57, 74-83, 88-94, 96-97, 101-104, 106-108, 110-111, 113-116, 119-123, 125-127, 129-135, 137-144, 147, 149, 151-152, 155-156, 162, 164, 170, 173-174, 177, 180-185, 187-189, 191, 193, 195-197, 200-201, 205, 209, 211-215, 217, 219, 221, 223
neutrality matters, 188
NGO, 188
NGOs, 171
NHWRU, 34
nimble, 41
NIS, 31, 185, 222

Niš, 71
node, 4, 52, 86, 105, 124, 135, 165, 170
nodes, 26
noise, 94, 146, 150
nonaligned, 24, 129
nonalignment, 11-12, 196
nonintervention, 15
nonmilitary, 95
Nonoften, 222
norm, 2, 73, 149
normalized, 22
norms, 3, 43, 71, 161, 221, 223
Norway, 25
nostalgia, 2, 53
nostalgic, 103
Notably, 168
notably, 61-62, 72, 91, 117
notion, 68, 82
notorious, 67
NPT, 11, 161, 222
nuance, 102
numerous, 158
nutrients, 156

O

Obama, 3
objection, 188
obligate, 98
obligated, 79
obligates, 89, 95, 161
obligating, 192
obligation, 15, 40, 81, 87, 89
obligations, 18, 31, 49, 62, 77, 90, 97, 101, 103, 105, 131, 134, 141-142, 147, 152, 161, 172, 180, 183-184, 192-193, 207, 219
obscure, 54, 72
observer, 79, 86
observers, 64, 68

obstacle, 81
obstruction, 95
occasional, 141
occupation, 65, 73, 118, 204
occupier, 75
oceanic, 146
October, 67, 195
oddities, 209
OECD, 112
Offences, 56
offences, 139
officer, 66
officers, 10, 34
officially, 9, 15-16, 30, 68
offshore, 21, 25
Oireachtas, 34, 43, 138, 140, 142, 180, 189, 216
ombudsman, 35
omission, 110, 159
omissions, 73
OneWeb, 99
opacity, 48, 146
operationally, 71
operatives, 95
opponents, 87
opportunist, 112
opposition, 161, 188-189
opt, 17, 81, 110, 193
opted, 53, 205
optic, 91
optics, 152
optout, 15
orbit, 99
orbits, 22
orchestrated, 33
ordnance, 150
org, 187-188
Organization, 164, 191, 222
organization, 68, 224
Organizations, 187-188

organizations, 51-52, 57, 64, 125, 200
oriented, 54, 101, 143, 156
Originally, 175
origins, 3, 40
outages, 99-100, 167, 169
outbreak, 181
outlaws, 224
outlets, 176
outlier, 112, 132
outlined, 143
Outlines, 183
outlines, 33
outlining, 98, 141-142, 221, 223
outpost, 19
outreach, 188
outsized, 85
outspoken, 189
outweigh, 131
overflights, 47
overfly, 204
overhaul, 193
Overlay, 115
overreach, 53, 62
overreliance, 113
overridden, 121, 209, 213
override, 25, 192, 216
Oversee, 214
oversee, 36
overseeing, 98, 176
Oversight, 211
oversight, 5, 35, 39, 48-49, 63, 73, 75, 139, 142, 157, 201, 203, 205, 209, 213-214, 216
overstepped, 67
overstretch, 67
overt, 9, 29, 80, 126
overtly, 47, 118
Overview, 203
overwhelm, 160
overwhelmed, 158, 171

ownership, 111

P

pacifism, 7
pacifist, 188
Pact, 10, 36, 61
pact, 14, 23, 74, 173, 193
pacts, 50, 138, 141
Palestinian, 208
PANA, 187, 189
pana, 187
panacea, 115
paradox, 27, 48
paralysed, 30, 33
paralyze, 130
paralyzed, 119
parameters, 73
paramilitaries, 64
Paris, 146-147, 150
Parliament, 189
parliament, 220
parliamentary, 21, 35, 39, 42, 49, 53, 102, 139, 142, 205, 214
parochial, 54
partially, 16, 160
participatory, 43, 49
particles, 220
partisanship, 132, 140
partly, 54
Partnership, 77, 80, 137, 182, 184, 192, 222
partnership, 40, 83, 135
partnerships, 22, 35, 48, 54, 102, 113, 118, 121
pathway, 3
patriotism, 3
patrols, 20, 25, 147, 150
pawn, 101, 114
peacebuilder, 18
peacebuilding, 14

peacefully, 56
peacekeepers, 46, 51, 53, 70, 172
Peacekeeping, 184, 223
peacekeeping, 3, 11, 13, 24, 40-41, 45, 48-50, 53, 55, 65, 70, 74, 77, 79, 87, 93, 104, 138, 142, 144, 147-148, 152, 170, 182-184, 188, 193, 196, 200-201, 205, 211, 224
peaceoriented, 196
peacetime, 160
penalties, 138-139, 142
peremptory, 221
peril, 102
periodic, 192
periphery, 19, 101, 172
perish, 173
perishable, 158
permanently, 146
perpetrators, 74
perpetual, 5
persisted, 15
personnel, 49, 89, 124, 159, 165, 172, 212
Persons, 20
perspective, 20, 66
persuasion, 102
PESCO, 18, 22-23, 36, 78, 80-81, 109, 137, 152, 168, 184, 188, 193, 197, 223
Pfizer, 130
PfP, 77-78, 182, 184, 192-193, 222
pharma, 131, 133
Pharmaceutical, 170
pharmaceutical, 4, 109, 111, 130-131, 134
philosophical, 1, 39
physically, 163
Picasso, 177
pierced, 107
piercing, 71

pillar, 36
pillars, 40, 157
pioneer, 152
pivotal, 47, 205
plagued, 142
planet, 151
planetary, 149, 152
plausible, 94, 118, 121, 125-126, 164
playbook, 33
players, 90
pledge, 78
pliable, 42
plunge, 157, 169
plunged, 67
pluralism, 53
podcasts, 54
poetry, 53, 57
poets, 51
polar, 26, 120
polarisation, 36
polarised, 172
polarising, 32
polarities, 3
polarization, 53
polarized, 10, 18
policymakers, 14, 41, 110, 205
policymaking, 102
politically, 9, 12, 23, 28, 35, 42, 48, 50, 56, 71, 82, 91, 97, 109, 162
politicians, 40, 96-97
politicization, 56
pollutants, 151
polluted, 153
polluters, 145
polluting, 151
pollution, 146, 149-150
populated, 63, 71, 203-204
portfolio, 113
portrayal, 112

possibilities, 98, 119, 147
postcrisis, 160
post militarised, 149
posture, 17, 23, 28, 47, 77, 82, 91, 94, 124, 132, 134, 142, 147, 161, 173
posturing, 155, 164, 193
potent, 27, 123
potentially, 91, 172, 192, 220
poverty, 112, 170, 172
POWs, 221
practicality, 9, 54
pragmatism, 7, 17, 47, 98
precarious, 55
precedent, 49, 64, 120-121, 146, 205
precedents, 207, 209
precisely, 18, 27, 47-48, 80, 92, 97, 102, 112, 133
precision, 175
precondition, 95
precursor, 220
predicament, 108, 119
predictability, 108, 129, 134
preemptive, 40
preferable, 98
premature, 170
premise, 130
premium, 113
preparation, 126
preparations, 142, 157
Preparedness, 223
preparedness, 4, 110, 119, 145, 147-148, 153, 155-157, 163
presence, 16, 22, 25, 66, 70, 72, 86, 109, 118, 199-200
preservation, 135, 180, 187, 191, 205
preserved, 88
preserving, 18, 200
President, 107, 117

prestige, 75
prestigious, 176
Presumption, 213
presumption, 139
pretexts, 56
prevailing, 158
prevention, 142
preventive, 196
previously, 23, 47, 49
priceless, 116
pride, 57, 93, 112, 152
primacy, 199-200
primarily, 29, 55, 61, 90, 96
Principle, 221
principle, 8-9, 17, 39, 42, 51, 54, 79-80, 82, 103, 110-111, 114, 116, 127, 138, 141, 144, 148, 162, 174, 179, 195, 211
principled, 11, 37, 74, 114, 125, 127, 143
principles, 26, 35, 43, 60, 62-63, 68, 71-72, 81, 102, 114-115, 125, 142-143, 179, 192, 195, 197
priorities, 77, 89, 121, 133
priority, 85, 113, 122, 160
prisoners, 70
Proactive, 26
proactive, 35, 112, 114, 123, 126, 140
probability, 170
probe, 34
problematic, 161
procedurally, 82
Procurement, 82
procurement, 36, 82, 109-110, 131, 133, 139, 148, 152, 193, 212
profile, 98, 133, 171
profound, 8, 15, 23, 123, 125, 168
progressive, 54, 132
Prohibition, 161, 195, 224
prohibition, 63, 73, 161-162, 208

projection, 79, 148, 152
PROJECTIONS, 163
Projections, 165, 219
projections, 4, 164, 168, 173
Proliferation, 11, 161, 222
proliferation, 161, 188
prolonged, 33, 68, 73, 167
prominent, 189
promotion, 46
prompted, 40, 62
pronounced, 14, 59
proof, 10, 46, 73, 103
propaganda, 64, 69
propellants, 150
Proponents, 63
proportionality, 63, 73, 162, 205
proportionally, 171
proportionate, 41, 98
prosecute, 73, 75
prosecutions, 55, 63, 70
prosperity, 90, 112, 135
protectionism, 107
protectionist, 111
protective, 101, 158
Protector, 67, 204
protector, 59
Protracted, 173
providers, 28, 94, 169
province, 70
provision, 162, 196
Provisions, 179, 200, 212, 216
provisions, 47, 98, 184, 197
provoke, 41, 60, 156
proxies, 66, 171
proximity, 21, 25, 62, 85, 166
Proxy, 170
proxy, 16, 29, 32, 52, 71, 170
psyche, 3, 8
psychiatry, 160
psychotherapy, 175
publications, 176

publicly, 112, 117, 155, 164
Publisher, 176
publisher, 176
pullouts, 213
punitive, 107, 111
pursuit, 126

Q

Qaeda, 65
quaint, 83, 97
quantify, 149

R

Račak, 64
radar, 21, 87
Radiation, 158
radiation, 156-158, 160, 164-165
radically, 159
Radiological, 223
radiological, 165, 167, 173
RAF, 21
Rahim, 208
Raisonné, 177
rallies, 111
rally, 48
rallying, 54
Ralph, 3
ramping, 25
ratification, 141, 184
ratified, 46, 161, 182
rationale, 46
rationing, 172
ravaged, 104
reactive, 30, 34, 123
reaffirms, 81, 115, 196, 200
realignment, 80, 88, 130
realism, 155, 163
realization, 56
reallocation, 112, 133

realm, 82, 123
reasonable, 91
reasserted, 105
rebalancing, 23, 113
rebel, 67-68, 205
rebellion, 180
rebels, 67
recalibrating, 131
recasts, 112
reciprocal, 31
reclaim, 112, 143
recognition, 32, 35, 73
recommendation, 196, 209
reconcile, 90, 147
reconciliation, 8, 71
reconfiguring, 24
reconsiderations, 130
reconsidered, 93, 124
reconsidering, 91
reconstituted, 31
Reconstruction, 160, 214
reconstruction, 8, 160, 200
reductions, 150
redundancy, 36, 93, 99-101, 105, 157
referenda, 102
Referendum, 213, 215, 217, 223
referendum, 5, 43, 80, 88, 90, 103, 134, 139, 141-143, 184, 188, 193, 212-213, 215-217
refineries, 146
reflex, 8
reform, 35-36, 42, 47-48, 57, 61, 73, 112
reforms, 31-32, 36, 47, 214
reframe, 112
refuel, 41
refueling, 47, 49, 85-86, 182
refuelling, 19, 166, 173
refuge, 158
refugee, 65, 165, 170, 172-173

Refugees, 171
refugees, 24, 167, 171
refusal, 2, 10, 14, 41-42, 83, 142, 144
regime, 59, 63, 67, 75, 107, 111, 203, 205
regimes, 69, 80, 130, 147
regional, 13-14, 21, 46, 66, 78, 99, 160
regionalised, 165
regionally, 105, 170
regulatory, 108-109, 122, 129, 134
reimagined, 55
reimagines, 35
reinterpretation, 43
reinterpreted, 82
reiterated, 14, 155
rejection, 137
Relevance, 193, 196, 209
relevance, 17, 47, 78, 207
Relevant, 179, 183-185, 191, 195
relevant, 52, 97, 131, 195, 199-200
reliability, 118, 134, 205
reliable, 125-126
reliance, 32, 59, 66, 87, 89, 156, 196
reliant, 21, 28, 169
relic, 1, 51, 104, 114, 135
relief, 41, 78
relocate, 111, 113
relocation, 33
reluctance, 23
remediation, 72
remedy, 73
remembrance, 53
reminder, 122
remit, 14, 59
remnants, 71
Rendition, 223

rendition, 68-69, 207, 209
renewable, 100
renewables, 148
renewal, 53, 143
renewed, 13-14, 51, 79, 127, 155
reopening, 8, 114
reorient, 156
reorientation, 89
reparations, 69
repatriate, 111
repeal, 142, 212
repeatedly, 9, 29, 86
reportedly, 30
repositioning, 86
representation, 69, 221
reprisal, 68
reprisals, 170
reproducing, 152
Republican, 15-16
repurposed, 85
repurposing, 4
reputation, 11, 50, 75, 101, 125, 143, 161, 175
reputational, 43, 82, 111, 115, 130-131
requirement, 40
rerouted, 93, 99
rerouting, 99
resemble, 75, 82
residue, 150
resilience, 34, 36, 95, 99, 110, 113, 122, 149, 152, 157, 160, 213, 220
resilient, 13, 37, 51, 53, 122, 124, 126, 148, 160
resistance, 7, 15, 33, 51, 53-54, 57, 94, 143
resistant, 36
Resisters, 188
resonated, 16
resonates, 102, 112

resourced, 98
respective, 176
respiratory, 160
responders, 158
Response, 34
response, 21-22, 24, 26, 29-31, 34-35, 40, 47, 60-61, 67, 77, 87, 89, 95, 110, 115, 118, 142, 147-148, 150, 152, 157-158, 192, 203, 219
responses, 25, 35, 87, 89, 95, 98, 146, 159, 213
responsibilities, 42, 70, 183
Responsibility, 63, 72, 94
responsibility, 49, 60, 68, 73, 82, 103, 116, 127, 149, 207
responsibly, 68
restrain, 75
restraint, 39, 43, 48, 79, 101, 205
restrictive, 41
resurgence, 66
resurging, 144
retaking, 66
retaliate, 30
retaliates, 169
retaliation, 20, 56, 79, 86-87, 89, 133, 212-213
retaliatory, 70, 90, 222
retiree, 97
retooling, 111
retreat, 55, 61, 116, 144
retrieve, 97
retrofitting, 158
retrospect, 68
reunified, 61
revenue, 108, 113
reversion, 160
revisit, 40
revisited, 103
revolution, 1
revolving, 105

rhetoric, 16, 92, 111, 148
rhetorical, 102, 126, 192
Rica, 116
rigorous, 47
rival, 10, 67, 101
rivalries, 11, 143
roadmap, 37
robust, 12, 17, 21, 43, 95, 118, 122, 126, 158, 209
robustness, 46
Roger, 189
rogue, 28, 112
Roma, 70
roughly, 131
routers, 92
routinely, 155
rubble, 74
rulesbased, 73
runoffs, 146
rupture, 7-8

S

sabotage, 20, 27, 32-34, 79, 86, 93, 95, 220
safeguard, 3, 17-18, 23, 39, 42, 57, 60, 79, 81, 98, 111, 123, 125-126, 130, 138, 205, 220
safeguarded, 51
safeguarding, 43, 92, 122, 212
Safeguards, 214
safeguards, 26, 80, 90, 209, 213, 215
safer, 3, 100
safest, 2
safety, 2, 56, 70, 92, 97, 105, 150, 180, 200
sake, 48, 163
sanction, 16
sanctioned, 40
Sanctions, 175, 212
sanctions, 87, 90, 109, 111, 115, 130, 134, 169, 182, 213
sanctuary, 107
satellite, 22-23, 25, 96, 99-100, 105, 158
Satellites, 22
satellites, 22, 100, 148
Saudi, 208
savvy, 132
Scam, 111
scam, 111-112
scarcity, 172
scaremongering, 155
scarred, 146
scars, 8
scenario, 118-123, 125, 127, 167-170, 172
scenarios, 4, 24, 100, 164, 166, 172-173, 183, 214
schism, 8
scholarly, 176
scholars, 22, 46, 54, 78
scientific, 22
scientist, 189
scorched, 146
scramble, 25
scrutinize, 4
scrutinized, 26
scrutinizes, 54
scrutiny, 14, 40, 42, 46, 60, 63, 81, 140, 151-152, 207
Sea, 21, 26, 95, 98, 168, 184, 221, 224
sea, 21, 24, 100, 149, 151, 166, 220
seabeds, 150
seaport, 97
seas, 152-153, 222
secondary, 158, 167-168, 172, 221
Secondly, 35

secretive, 112, 212, 223
Security, 12, 14, 23, 28, 31, 34, 40-41, 48-49, 59, 62-67, 70, 72-73, 75, 81, 90, 142, 148, 161, 182, 184, 195-196, 199, 201, 203, 216, 219, 224
security, 13-15, 17, 23, 25, 29, 35-37, 41, 43, 47, 52-53, 55-56, 59, 61, 63, 68-69, 74, 78-79, 85-87, 89-91, 95-96, 99, 102-103, 105-106, 109, 115, 118-126, 131-134, 141, 145-147, 149, 152, 156, 177, 191, 195-196, 199-200, 219, 221, 223-224
seductive, 5, 96
Selective, 223
selective, 15, 65, 68, 72, 74
selfdefense, 65
selfdetermination, 125
sensitive, 23, 27, 29-30, 61, 146, 168, 172
sensory, 69
sentiment, 4, 13, 16, 131
sentimentality, 3
separately, 152
September, 9, 60, 65, 207
Serbian, 64-65, 70
Serbs, 70
seriously, 105
seriousness, 70
settlement, 134, 179
sever, 93
severed, 100
severely, 118
severity, 139, 212
shadowy, 93
Shannonwatch, 187, 189
shannonwatch, 187
shareholders, 112
shattered, 164
shatters, 74

sheltering, 156, 159
Sheraton, 176
shield, 4, 24, 94, 104, 115, 138, 156, 164, 196, 219
shielded, 63, 69, 107, 151
Shielding, 212
shields, 125
shipments, 108
shipyards, 146
shortages, 156, 160, 167, 171, 173
showcases, 176
sickness, 158
sideline, 121
sidelined, 126
sidelines, 119, 133
siege, 1, 108-109
signatories, 69
signatory, 22, 81, 95, 98, 161, 184-185, 193
silence, 69, 96, 101, 103, 112, 137, 155
silent, 157
silos, 35
Similarly, 118, 122, 148
similarly, 36
simplicity, 96
Simply, 109
simply, 7, 11, 39-40, 82, 100, 126, 174
Simultaneously, 109
simultaneously, 109
sincerity, 63
Singapore, 31, 36, 113, 116, 130
Sirte, 67
situation, 163
situational, 22
skepticism, 103
skirmish, 97
sleight, 92, 101, 103
Slobodan, 64
slogans, 116

slurs, 115
sobering, 115, 163
socialists, 16
softening, 33
soldier, 99
soldiers, 3, 9-10, 39, 41, 49, 100
solidarity, 2, 13, 15, 48, 50, 54, 60, 114, 118
solution, 95, 98, 102
solutions, 8, 98
someday, 14
Sonar, 150
sonar, 146, 150
sorties, 64
soundbites, 111
southwest, 21
Sovereign, 132
sovereign, 2, 20, 29, 31, 49, 63, 65, 73, 80, 108, 121, 127
SOVEREIGNTY, 137
Sovereignty, 5, 35, 138, 140-141, 143, 209, 211-212, 215, 221, 223
sovereignty, 5, 7-10, 14, 17-18, 21-23, 27, 29-30, 32, 35-36, 39, 53, 63, 76, 80, 83, 87, 90, 92, 95, 101, 106, 111, 114-116, 118-120, 122-128, 133, 137-138, 143-144, 149, 152, 156-157, 160, 162, 181, 185, 197, 208-209, 213, 220, 222
Soviet, 10, 12-13, 33, 60-61, 74
SpaceX, 22
spanning, 149
sparked, 67
sparse, 117
species, 146
spectacle, 2
specter, 40
spectre, 95, 97
speculation, 163
speculative, 27, 94, 125, 164
speech, 2, 55

speeches, 57, 111, 176
sphere, 28, 62, 119
spillover, 173
spiral, 169
spite, 131
sprawling, 65, 146, 150
Springfield, 176
spy, 22
stabilization, 67
stabilize, 65
stabilizing, 46, 48, 70
staggering, 146
stakeholder, 25, 79, 88
stance, 2, 8, 15, 20, 22, 28, 37, 52, 74, 91, 102, 110, 122-123, 130, 151, 162, 180, 185, 187
standardize, 78
standoff, 10
standoffs, 20
standpoint, 40
staple, 155
Starlink, 99
starvation, 165, 221
statebuilding, 65
statecraft, 3, 79, 108
stateless, 208
statesponsored, 28
static, 13
statistics, 164
status, 24, 26, 28, 32, 86, 88, 122, 129, 131, 138, 140, 157, 162, 192, 221
Statute, 33, 43, 49, 184, 223
statute, 34, 80, 141
statutory, 31, 35, 56, 142
steadfast, 127
steadily, 33, 77
steady, 96, 131
steward, 151
stewardship, 99, 125, 152
stifle, 2

stockpile, 155
stockpiles, 158, 173
stockpiling, 147, 156, 185
stopovers, 137
storytelling, 54, 176
straddling, 28
strandings, 150
STRATEGIC, 85
Strategic, 62, 109, 113, 126, 156, 223
strategic, 1, 4, 17, 19-21, 24, 29-30, 34, 40-41, 47, 50-51, 61-62, 66-67, 74, 77-80, 82-83, 85-90, 92, 94, 101-102, 104, 107-108, 110-111, 114-115, 117-126, 129-130, 132-133, 135, 144, 151, 164, 166, 168, 173, 193, 213, 220
Strategically, 90
strategically, 9, 69, 91, 224
streamline, 41
strength, 41-42, 48, 53-54, 76, 100, 106, 135, 143
strengths, 74
strictly, 81
stronghold, 53
strongmen, 66-67
structural, 14, 63, 90, 113
Submarine, 87, 224
submarine, 20, 27, 94-95, 98, 150-151
submission, 104
Subpoena, 140
subpoena, 213
subservience, 2
substantive, 52
subtle, 79, 123
subtler, 1, 109
subtly, 77
subversive, 33
subverts, 32
suicide, 168, 170

superfluous, 162
Supermajority, 213
superpower, 11, 55, 104, 113
superpowers, 10
supervised, 35
supporter, 13
Supporters, 61, 66, 79
supporters, 161
suppress, 56
supranational, 53, 55, 83
supremacy, 74
Supreme, 141, 213
surely, 115
surrounding, 19, 47, 55, 72, 167
surveil, 56
surveillance, 19-22, 26, 56, 75, 86-87, 96-97, 124, 150-151, 162, 166, 184, 214
SURVIVAL, 155
survival, 104, 115, 156-157, 159-160, 174, 219
susceptible, 158
Suspension, 196
suspicion, 7, 50
sustain, 82
sustainability, 66, 147-149, 152, 188
sway, 224
Sweden, 13, 17, 29, 131
swiftly, 41, 59, 99
symbol, 59, 66
symbolically, 43
sympathetic, 16
sympathies, 16
systemic, 28, 172
systemically, 213

T

tactical, 66, 74
Tactics, 32

tactics, 3, 33, 56, 95, 146, 221
tailored, 126, 156
tainted, 69
tale, 119, 126
talent, 130
Taliban, 65-66
Tallinn, 28, 31, 224
Tánaiste, 47
tandem, 103
tangible, 36, 39, 53, 75, 133
tankers, 66
Taoiseach, 9, 36, 181
tariff, 107, 114-115
Tariffs, 115
tariffs, 2, 4, 108-109, 111, 114, 213
Tech, 93, 130, 134
tech, 4, 28, 32, 86, 90, 99, 105-106, 109, 113, 130, 132, 168, 170-171
technicality, 39
technically, 47, 72, 78, 121
techniques, 68
technocrats, 51
technological, 74, 92, 99, 102, 120, 124, 169
technologically, 37
technologies, 29, 79, 87, 117, 120, 126, 148
technology, 22, 54, 57, 88, 92-94, 124
teeth, 139, 212
telecom, 94, 167, 169
telecommunications, 22, 98, 224
telecoms, 160
Telehealth, 169
temporarily, 109
tempted, 9, 42
tenable, 164
tension, 14, 23, 29, 60, 167

tensions, 8, 32, 42, 55, 73, 86, 105, 150, 156
terrain, 72, 146
territorial, 21, 59, 61, 150, 195, 220, 222, 224
territories, 117, 192
territory, 20-21, 24, 26, 32, 46, 49, 119, 123-124, 142, 162, 204, 207-209, 211, 216
Terror, 68
Terrorism, 170
terrorism, 41, 56, 59, 69, 79, 170-172, 207
terrorist, 65-66, 172
testimonies, 209
textbook, 68, 201
THE ART MARKET, 176
theater, 89
theaters, 40
theatre, 25, 165, 168-169
theatres, 164
theft, 27, 32
theoretical, 4, 33, 86
theories, 219
theory, 3, 45
therapy, 175
thorough, 177
threat, 3, 13, 16, 21, 24, 28, 35, 61-62, 86, 90, 92, 94-95, 97-99, 101-103, 105, 151, 158, 162, 172, 192, 195, 203-204, 222
threaten, 24, 129
threatened, 2, 9, 111
threatening, 3, 50, 81, 150
threats, 18, 27, 29-30, 33-35, 41, 52, 59, 79, 94-95, 98, 102, 106, 108, 110-111, 115, 121-122, 124, 126, 143, 149, 155, 157, 163, 168, 185, 203, 213, 220, 222
threshold, 28, 32, 40, 80, 89-90, 122

thresholds, 30, 35, 213
Thule, 118
thyroid, 158, 221
tides, 126
Tier, 165-167, 169-171
Tiered, 219
tiers, 165
Timeline, 181
Timor, 46
toll, 59, 73, 149, 163, 172-173
tone, 57
topics, 175
topography, 99
topsoil, 159
Torture, 69
torture, 68-69, 207-208
tortured, 208
toxins, 151
TPNW, 161-162, 224
tragedies, 53
tragedy, 9
transatlantic, 3, 19, 85-86, 88-89, 92, 104, 119, 124, 166
transboundary, 167
transcends, 145
transit, 85, 161
Transitional, 216
transits, 5
transmission, 92
transmit, 22, 97
Transparency, 122, 125, 160
transparency, 35, 63, 70, 78, 103, 119, 140, 205, 209
transportation, 172
trauma, 8, 17, 160, 164-165, 167, 173
trawlers, 93
Treaties, 183
treaties, 26, 30, 52, 73, 95, 118, 140, 144, 161, 213, 219, 221

Treaty, 8, 11-12, 14-15, 17, 22-24, 60, 81, 108, 110, 161, 180, 182-184, 191-193, 219, 222, 224
treaty, 24, 28, 55, 60-61, 72, 77, 81, 87, 90, 141-142, 161-162, 183, 191, 193, 216, 221-223
tri, 81
tribal, 67
tripling, 108
triumph, 5
troop, 97, 135, 151
troops, 11, 42, 46, 48-50, 81-82, 97, 168, 182, 195-196, 199-200, 205, 224
truest, 144
truly, 100
Trump, 2, 4, 107, 117
trumps, 112
truth, 2, 15, 91, 104, 170, 174
turbulence, 40
twin, 129
twofold, 24
twotier, 114

U

UHNWI, 176
Ultra, 176
unaligned, 106
unambiguously, 41
unarmed, 34
Unauthorised, 212
unauthorized, 21, 56, 200
unbound, 2
UNCLOS, 21, 95, 98, 184, 221, 224
unconstitutional, 139, 212
uncovered, 68
underbelly, 91
undercurrent, 117
underdeveloped, 28

underdiscussed, 133
underequipped, 173
underestimated, 89
underfunded, 62, 98
underpinned, 12, 114, 131
underpinning, 7, 43, 91, 197
underpinnings, 17
underpins, 195
underreported, 149
underresourced, 28
underscore, 30, 42, 209
underscored, 15-16
underscores, 170, 196, 205
underscoring, 192
UNDERSEA, 91
Undersea, 20, 224
undersea, 4, 20-21, 85-87, 91-94, 98, 100-101, 106, 157, 169, 184, 224
understaffed, 173
underwater, 92, 150
underway, 103
underwritten, 109
unease, 11, 40, 78
unenforceable, 28
Uneven, 223
unexploded, 71-72, 150
unfamiliar, 99
unfold, 32, 48, 118, 122
unfolding, 25, 62, 80, 125
unguarded, 115
UNIFIL, 45, 49, 224
unilateral, 3, 39, 63, 108, 200
unilateralism, 74
unilaterally, 81, 112
unintended, 29
uninterrupted, 131, 169
unionists, 16
uniquely, 17, 27-28, 93-94, 102, 132, 156
unity, 9, 62

unlawful, 82, 207, 209
unlivable, 152
unmandated, 39
UNMIK, 65
unofficial, 16
unprecedented, 110
unprepared, 157
unpunished, 32
unregulated, 75, 150-151
unrelated, 48
unreliable, 69
unrest, 170
UNSC, 63, 199, 201, 203, 205
unsent, 135
unsettled, 71
unstable, 134
untenable, 114
unthinkable, 155
unveiled, 148
unwavering, 10, 125, 128
unwilling, 11, 119
unwillingness, 70
upcoming, 176
upheaval, 174
uprising, 67, 203
urgency, 52, 62, 95
usage, 100

V

vagueness, 83
Valera, 9-10, 16, 181
valuesdriven, 50
vaults, 159
vehicle, 96
veil, 101
ventilation, 158
venture, 113
ventures, 79, 132, 134
verified, 94
vested, 99

veterans, 51, 57
veto, 41, 48
vetted, 112
viable, 98, 123, 160
victim, 71
victims, 69, 73
victories, 3
Vienna, 12
vigilance, 48, 53, 122, 209
vigilant, 126
VII, 43, 49, 203
vilify, 111
VILLIAN, 59
violation, 21, 30, 42, 63, 72, 115, 121, 207, 209
violations, 4, 33, 49, 69, 95, 124, 139, 209, 212
violence, 53, 64, 70
voiding, 20
voters, 111
vying, 67

W

Wallace Mick, 189
WARFARE, 27
Warfare, 34, 220-221
warfare, 4, 20, 25, 27, 32-35, 37, 41, 52-53, 79, 83, 86, 89, 95, 111, 122, 144-145, 162, 168, 214, 219-221
warfighting, 62, 70, 75
warlord, 66
warrant, 49
warranting, 121
Warsaw, 10, 61
warships, 21, 94, 100
wartime, 9, 34, 70, 88, 158, 180
Warzones, 146
watchdog, 140, 187, 212
watchdogs, 54

waterboarding, 69
watershed, 64
waypoint, 46
wealth, 132
Weapon, 165, 223
weapon, 52, 111, 188
Weaponised, 224
weaponization, 107
weaponized, 94, 111
weaponry, 71-72, 74
Weapons, 11, 146, 161, 222, 224
weapons, 5, 49-50, 63, 71-73, 78-79, 82, 146-147, 149-150, 161-162, 222, 224
Whistleblower, 212
whistleblower, 139
wildfires, 149
Withdrawal, 192
withdrawal, 12, 65-66, 113, 187, 200
workforce, 132-133
worldwide, 188
WRI, 188
writer, 176
WWII, 17, 181
www, 187-188

Y

yield, 33, 96
yielding, 10
youth, 54, 57
youthful, 54

Z

Zubaydah, 208
UNIFIL (Lebanon) – 55, 205
Veto powers (UN Security Council) – 202–204
Whistleblower protections –

145–146, 216
World War II (Irish neutrality) –
10–11, 189

www.ingramcontent.com/pod-product-compliance
Lightning Source LLC
Chambersburg PA
CBHW050857160426
43194CB00011B/2184